The Elders Speak

Two Psychologists Share
Their Lifetimes of Experience

The Elders Speak

Two Psychologists Share
Their Lifetimes of Experience

Editor: Bruce R. Mulkey

Cover photograph: Phyllis W. Moffitt

Cover design: David Lynch, Lynch Graphics

Published by Lulu Press

Printed in the United States of America

First Edition

ISBN 978-0-557-81628-6

Barbara — I look back through time and still see your beautiful countenance. I look today and it's still there! And I have always looked up to you!

Jo E Hoover

The Elders Speak

Two Psychologists Share

Their Lifetimes of Experience

Eli Mitchell

By Ellison C. Mitchell, Ph.D.
and
John E. Hoover, Ph.D.

Jo E Hoover

Acknowledgements

To the women who sourced my anima . . .

Mom, Kitty, Hessie, Mrs. McBee, "Essie G.," Aunt Mary Lou, Beverly, Ma Ma Mitchell, Martha P., Nancy L., Irma Lee, Nanne, Ann Cleveland, Tina, and Lucy; most of all, Lucy.

—Eli Mitchell

First, I (John Hoover) want to acknowledge my high school classmates who touched my life without knowing that I wanted to grow up to be like them: Mike Batton (deceased) enthusiastic, loyal, no pretenses; David Crary, self-reliant, witty, bright, clever; Ken Graham, respectable, competent, authentic; Marcina Hehr Mason, brilliant, sensitive, beautiful . . . who set the standard for all other women in the world; Jim Huffman, wise, accepting, generous, and gentle; Larry Lehman, liked by everybody because he liked everybody; Barbara Myers Emerson, poised, graceful, elegant; David Phillips, understanding, unselfish, and my earliest friend in life whose friendship still remains.

To all of my clients who have been my greatest teachers.

I want to acknowledge programs that have had a major influence in my professional work:

- The University of Texas's Psychology Internship under the direction of Dr. Ira Iscoe, whose fatherly influence on me provided a great boost to my career as a professional psychologist.

- Don Richard Riso and Russ Hudson, authors and presenters in the use of the Enneagram Personality Inventory. Their system makes a lot of sense. I use it with all my clients.

- The More to Life Foundation was created by Brad Brown and Roy Whitten. My experiences in that program, including the processes I learned in their trainings, made it possible for me to discover my self. I also acknowledge the entire body of trainers who deliver the life-changing experiences that can awaken people to discover their highest noble selves. They deliver the training with such elegance and rock-solid basic tools of personal transformation that it continues to leave me awe-inspired every single time I participate as a support member on a training team.

I want to acknowledge Champions in my personal and professional life who fuel my soul: David Hoffman, brilliant, funny, profound; John Koehler, teacher, spiritualist, adventurist, woodsman; Steve DeWitt, the wisest person I know; Mary Bledsoe, kind, solid, thoughtful; Eli Mitchell, my open and gentle co-author; Vergil Metts, brilliant, creative, indefatigable professional; Bobby Carr, insightful, dependable, and emotionally intelligent; Sharon Allaman Hoover, my beautiful life-partner and wife and the reason I love life. She is simply the most honest, responsible, and powerful force for good that I know. In the words of Tom Paxton's song "My Lady's a Wild Flying Dove:" ". . . she tells me she's learnin' how full her cup can be, she asks me to help her, but I know she's teachin' me . . ."

And, a big acknowledgement to Bruce Mulkey, dear friend and editor, for the guidance, persevering, prodding, and shepherding without which we could not have completed our intention to write this book.

–John Hoover

Table of Contents

Foreword

Together, authors Eli Mitchell and John Hoover have 75 years of experience as psychologists, working with individuals, couples, families, and groups. For a number of years, they teamed up to lead Gestalt group training experiences for professionals in the mental health fields. And as friends for 32 years, they have spent many hours together discussing their observations and thoughts about mind, body, and soul. Now, as elders in the psychotherapeutic community, they have chosen to share some of their observations and knowledge with a broader audience.

In this book, Mitchell and Hoover share some of the processes, concepts, and techniques they employ; testimony and stories of clients who have benefited from their expertise; and some of the authors' own experiences of personal growth.

While they take their professional work very seriously, Mitchell and Hoover strive to maintain their balance by refusing to take themselves too seriously. They agree, "The more we know, the more we discover we don't know."

For more about Eli Mitchell and John Hoover, see "About the Authors."

PATHS TO EMOTIONAL HEALTH,

INSIGHT, AND POSITIVE CHANGE

The levels at which we function

John Hoover

Before there were self-help sections in book stores, before pop psychology or avant-garde spiritual literature became featured as books of the month, I stumbled across a book, *The Lazy Man's Guide to Enlightenment*, written by Thaddeus Golas. At the time I chuckled and dismissed it as "cute" but naïve and unscientific. Yet thirty-some years later, I see the influence that book has had on my philosophy of personal-spiritual development. It got me thinking.

Golas spoke of people vibrating at different frequencies, contracting and expanding, thus experiencing the world differently depending on which level of vibration they were on. Golas believed that in the expanded state, when people were vibrating very fast, they would sense themselves as being at their best, really on top of things because they would be vibrating relatively faster than the customary normal vibration level of the rest of the world. As such, their thinking and actions would appear to be moving faster than the normal rate for human beings.

Conversely he believed that when we were at our worst, we were vibrating slower relative to the rest of the world and were in a contracted state of being. On those days, everything would seem to have gotten ahead of us. We just wouldn't be able to think or move fast enough to keep up. Golas gave an example of sitting at an outdoor café. At the table next to him as the person got up to leave, the table tipped and the coffee cup fell off the table. Golas saw it out of the corner of his eye reached down and caught the cup in mid air and set it back on the table. Golas realized that there are days when that same exact event could have occurred and the cup would have fallen to the sidewalk and broken into a thousand pieces before he'd moved a muscle. He must have sensed that he was in one of those expanded states that morning and was vibrating faster relative to the normal vibration of the world.

Often people talk about having good days and bad days. But, what makes them so? Is it the day itself? Or, is it the person's state of mind that makes it good or bad? Perhaps one's state of contraction or expansion determines what kind of meanings our automatic mind makes the day out to be.

We know that people unknowingly and automatically ascribe judgments of right/wrong, good/bad, should/shouldn't to the everyday things that happen every day. Whatever life-event happens every day is just . . . life, life-as-it-is. At the most fundamental level, life-events are neutral, but how each person perceives such events will differ greatly. The events that life gives us are largely out of our control. But, what perceptions, what meanings that WE give to the events are exactly what we can control—or can learn to control. When we can do that, we can begin to determine the quality of life that we really want to have. But first we have to know that our "automatic mind" is judging, criticizing, approving, and disapproving, moment by moment, day in and day out.

Even though every psychology student studies several theories and models of cognitive therapy, I learned the most about the internal patterns of thinking, by participating in many intensive weekend training experiences in the More to Life program. One of the processes in the training utilizes a cognitive process that is called the clearing process. This process reveals that the human mind reacts to life-events by creating (in a fraction of a second) a whole bunch of beliefs, judgments, and predictions, most of which are false and most of which are outside of our conscious awareness. However false they may be, these beliefs can evoke strong negative feelings within us. For example, consider a time when you were having a "bad" day and didn't even know why! The clearing process is designed to help people discern truths from the false beliefs, which, of course, are the ones most responsible for our negative feelings, and to then correct the cognitive errors and make new decisions based on data verified to be true.

I have experienced a number of training programs over the years including several on the Enneagram personality types as developed by Don Riso and Russ Hudson:

> *Identifying oneself as one of nine personality types can be revolutionary. For the first time in our lives, we may see the pattern and overall rationale for the way we have lived and behaved.*

> *The modern Enneagram of personality type . . . is a condensation of universal wisdom, the perennial philosophy accumulated by Christians, Buddhists, Muslims (especially the Sufis), and Jews (in the Kabbalah) for thousands of years. . . . Beneath surface differences and appearances, behind the veils of illusion, the light of Divinity shines in every individual.*

> —The *Wisdom of the Enneagram*, Riso & Hudson, Bantam Books, 1999.

There are several Enneagram authors and teachers. Don Riso and Russ Hudson's model includes levels of development—healthy to unhealthy—as well as thorough descriptions of the behavior patterns of each of the nine personality types of the Enneagram.

Riso and Hudson's model shows how differently a particular personality type behaves according to what level of development (functioning) that personality type is operating on. So if your personality is identified as being The Reformer, for example, it's important to know that the Reformer's patterns change predictably when they move up or down the levels of development. Just knowing the type is not sufficient. You must also know: Are you at your type's best level? Or are you somewhere down the levels in an unhealthy pattern characteristic of your personality type?

As I was studying with Riso and Hudson I would occasionally think about Thaddeus Golas's expansion and contraction model that describes people as ever expanding and contracting, like a flower opening and closing each day. It reminded me of how we see that people move up and down the levels of development every day.

In the Enneagram model, the three basic levels of development—(1) healthy, (2) average, and (3) unhealthy—are each further subdivided into three sublevels for a total of nine levels of development. Each level is identified by Riso and Hudson as follows:

- Healthy: Level 1: Level of Liberation
- Healthy: Level 2: Level of Psychological Capacity
- Healthy: Level 3: Level of Social Value

- Average: Level 4: Level of Imbalance
- Average: Level 5: Level of Interpersonal Control
- Average: Level 6: Level of Overcompensation

- Unhealthy: Level 7: Level of Violation/Addiction
- Unhealthy: Level 8: Level of Delusion/Compulsion
- Unhealthy: Level 9: Level of Pathological Destructiveness

At each level of development we perceive the world, or reality, through the "filters" of our mind. At our best at Level 1, the ego is "transparent." We are open, present, spontaneous, wise, and resourceful. Ego's defenses are not contaminating our view of reality. We are not resisting life-as-it-is. We are connected with what is happening in our here-and-now moment and our true self, our Essence, is most revealed. I feel certain that Thaddeus Golas would recognize this as the condition of expanded beings.

At Levels 2 and 3, we continue to function in a healthy way though our freedom to think and choose our actions begins to become constrained by the ego patterns and the structures of the personality type. We begin to shift toward identifying ourselves in a fixed role.

With each descending level, more layers of defenses are added to cope with the increased fears. As we spiral downward (disintegrate) we experience more extensive distortions of reality and more fears. Ironically we may not even notice any changes within us. We think we are just responding clearly and appropriately to the circumstances going on around us. To us, our feelings and thoughts match the disposition of the life-events. But that is not what is true. What is true is that we react to life-events according to the level of development we are in at the time of the event. The level of development determines the meanings one's mind will make up about the life event.

At Levels 4, 5, and 6, according to Riso and Hudson, we are in the Average range of the levels of development. This is the range of functioning at which we find most of us most of the time. Though the behaviors exhibited are "normal" behaviors for that personality type, our full potential is considerably constricted. We almost completely identify ourselves with our ego with increasing egocentricity as we move to the lower range of "normal," continuing to do so as we enter the unhealthy levels. The spontaneous wisdom, compassion, and strength of Level 1 is gone as is our ability to respond to life in an emotionally healthy manner. The mid-range between expanded beings and contracted beings, Thaddeus Golas called "massed beings."

The unhealthy levels of development, Levels 7, 8, and 9, are usually entered into from the lower end of the normal levels due to some major life catastrophe. I tend to think of the healthy levels as being characterized as the "being for" zone, and the unhealthy levels as the "being against" zone. The being against zone is characterized by intense fright and intense anger (fight or flight). At these levels, we are in a state of constriction, reaction, and obsession. The ego is out of touch with reality. Major personality disorders, psychosis, and even death can result at these levels. Thaddeus Golas would certainly recognize this to be that "contracted state of being."

It has been my experience that people at their best have not one ounce of "againstness" in them. They are typically open, loving, flexible, wise, calm, compassionate, strong, involved, alive, creative, and inspiring, in a word, "FOR." We humans even have the capacity to freely sacrifice our lives for the lives of others. At our very best we are "FOR" the whole of humanity, the highest good for all. All of us have this highest level of development inside ourselves. In fact, it is the nature of our true self, our very Essence.

The big question: "What do you do when you realize that you are not at your higher-level self?" When we are in a contracted state, Thaddeus said to love yourself. Huh? Now that's a stunner! Love myself when I am jammed, hostile, and blaming? Love yourself for being jammed, hostile, and blaming! What? Yep, that's what he said. Didn't make any sense to me! Truly love yourself as you are in that state of contraction, and you will expand into a higher level. That's what he said! And, over the years I have come to know that those words are absolutely true. I know from my experience. Somewhere early on in my years as a psychologist I began a journey to solve the mystery Thaddeus posed for me: "How do you do it? How do you love yourself when you don't feel even one bit of self love?" That's the question that launched me on a journey to find some answers.

I read the Bible and biblical books. I have meditated at the ashram with the Guru. I have been drawn to spiritual discourses and practices. Eli Mitchell and I have spent many hours in discussions about the spiritual life. With two other special friends, John Koehler and Steve DeWitt (the wisest man I know) we regularly spend time together in the wilderness in spiritual retreats. I read the *Daily Dharma*. Doesn't everybody feel drawn to explore that "higher ground" once they've experienced even a moment of its humbling, thrilling vibration? We know there is something beyond our ego identification.

Recently in the *Daily Dharma*, I read the following answer given by Shinzen Young to the question: What is the ego?

Through consistent practice we develop the skill of mindfulness, which allows us to detect with great precision the often subtle self-referential ideas and body sensations as they arise in each act of perception. We also develop equanimity so that we can allow these ideas and body sensations to expand and contract without suppression, interference, or clinging. Eventually, contact with the sense of self becomes so continuous that there is no time left to congeal or fixate it. The self then becomes clarified in the sense that it is no longer experienced as an opaque, rigid, ever-present entity, but rather as a transparent, elastic, vibratory activity. It loses 'thingness.' We realize that it is a verb, not a noun; a wave, not a particle. According to this paradigm, what is let go of is the unconsciousness and 'holding' associated with those ideas and body sensations which produce a sense of self. The sense of self becomes a home rather than a prison. You can come and go freely.

–Shinzen Young, "What Does Being a Buddhist Mean to You?" (Fall 1993) *Tricycle: The Buddhist Review.*

Does this not sound familiar! . . . from Thaddeus Golas, Riso & Hudson, and a host of others journeying on paths of seeking life's evolution of higher consciousness?

As a starting point I think a good question to ask ourselves when we're feeling upset is: "What do I believe about this situation that is causing me to feel upset?" Only when I can objectively discern the truthfulness or falseness of my belief and therefore discern the level of development at which I perceive the situation, do I have the chance to shift and move up to a higher level of development, to move from a contracted state to an expanded state, from "Against-ness" to "For-ness" . . . including for myself and for others' highest good.

Speaking the truth in love

Eli Mitchell

One of my favorite Scriptures is in Paul's letter to the Ephesians (4:15): "Rather, let our lives lovingly express truth in all things." The following episode illustrates the importance of speaking the truth in love, especially to children.

I did my year-long clinical psychology internship at a child guidance clinic in Los Angeles. Working with many types of families—broken, blended, multicultural, et cetera—under supervision was an outstanding learning experience.

A middle class mother brought in her nine-year-old son with a concern that he was depressed. First, I interviewed Mom alone, and she described Billy as a good boy who for several weeks had been "apathetic about everything," had lost his appetite, and seemed unusually tired and moody. Eventually, in whispers the mother revealed that her husband had been in prison for two months serving a six-month sentence for embezzlement. When asked, she admitted the father's absence might be contributing to her son's depression, but she doubted it. She went on to explain that she thought Billy believed her story that Dad was on an extra-long business trip and would be back in a few months.

Next I talked to Billy by himself and got a surprise when his father's absence came up. "I know he's dead," the dejected boy said. "Mom just can't tell me, so I'm playing along. He died somehow I'm sure."

Back to talking to Mom (by herself) again, I convinced her that Billy's disturbance most probably came from his assuming the worst about his fathers absence, that is, he was dead. She agreed to let me coach her on how to tell Billy the truth in love.

I invited Billy back into the counseling room, this time along with his mother. Mom did a great job conveying the real story. She told Billy his dad was very much alive and that he did something wrong; he stole some money, and he had to go to jail for six months. She had lied to him to prevent him from feeling bad. Now she realized it had confused him rather than helped him, and she was very sorry.

As his mother spoke, Billy's faced showed disbelief, slow belief, relief, and then tears—tears of joy.

Mom and son hugged. She continued by saying they could call him and even visit him, if Billy wanted to, which he certainly did.

Billy asked one more question, "Will dad be home for Christmas?" Mom stood up and gave a resounding, "Yes!"

They parted my office, arms around each other.

If children (and perhaps all of us) don't hear the truth, they tend to create a "worse case" scenario. Speaking the truth in love to kids includes making sure they understand the truth and telling them only as much as they want to know at that time.

Being and doing

John Hoover & Eli Mitchell

Eli: I was thinking about the concept of "polarities" that Fritz Perls so frequently introduced in Gestalt groups, as a way to help us become aware of internal conflicts. People have so many splits, straddling the fence on important issues in their lives. People can flip their "world view" from one polar end to its opposite when they have not balanced or integrated those opposing views.

John: Yeah, I hear myself at times saying, "On the one hand . . . but on the other hand . . ."

Eli: And sometimes people say, "A part of me wants one thing . . . but another part of me says 'No, no, no!'" Perls maintained that there are some universal polarities that show up in just about everybody. Can you think of an example of work you've done with a client with a dramatic polarity?

John: Virtually every client that I see recognizes the internal struggle within them between the drivenness to succeed, on the one hand, and a need to feel contentment and self-acceptance just as they are, on the other hand. I think everybody experiences some duality inside regarding such common polarities as "top dog versus bottom dog," "masculine energy versus feminine energy," "good boy versus bad boy," "driven to accomplish (doing) versus I am complete and whole just as I am (being)."

For example, a guy named Marcus came to see me for therapy. He was a young engineer who had been working in a technical field pretty successfully but who was also fairly uncomfortable with others in the work group. He had always been self motivated, disciplined, and productive but kept pretty much to himself. Nine months prior to his coming in Marcus was promoted to the position of a first-line supervisor. Soon he began dreading going to work, feeling like a fish out of water, overwhelmed and uncertain as to what to do.

Eli: Boy, that's an old story isn't it! In one step that company lost a good engineer and gained a bad manager!

John; Yeah, Human Resources made the referral to me. Marcus wanted some information to understand the problem so he could figure out what he could do.

Eli: Oh, yes. He wanted it all to be rational.

John: Of course. So I gave him a rational, cognitive model for his left brain to deal with, but a model that illustrates the right brain—the emotional, relationship, feeling side as well: the Being-Doing model.

Eli: That's a good way to start, appeal to his head since that's what he uses most of the time, and then a little later to the heart side, the side that really needs to see the light of day for a change! Tell me how you use that Being-Doing model with clients in your office.

John: On my white board in my office, I draw a line to divide the board vertically in the middle. Then, a few inches from the top, I draw a horizontal line intersecting the vertical line. On the top, left side I write the word "Being." On the top right side I write the word "Doing."

"Doing" represents a process of actions that it takes to progress from starting point A, to reach a goal at point B. This signifies some achievement, progress, or success that can be measured objectively.

"Being" represents quality of experience whether or not there is any goal to reach. It is thought of more in qualitative terms than quantitative. Since experience is not a behavioral, observable activity, it is not measured by monitoring what you are doing. In fact, you could say "being" refers to how you are doing what you are doing.

Since "driven to doing" is about making progress, achieving, succeeding, growing, and developing, the focus is future-oriented. Action steps are developed and then acted upon in order to reach the goal, and metrics are usually used to define one's progress.

Eli: This is the side that would appeal to Marcus.

John: Oh yeah. "Being" is present-centered experience. It is the experience of one's self, one's experience of others, and one's experience of the context of life that exists in each moment. Context of life means the situation, the circumstances, the facts, the events that are happening in the moment, including your intentions and your objectives.

It is in the "being" state that we can create a better, healthier quality of our experience of our life. It is a choice we can make about how we are being as we do what we're doing. It is our attitude, a kind of mental-emotional posture toward the subject about which we are taking action. When someone asks, "How are you doing?" They most often mean, "How are you feeling?" The question concerns the quality of one's state of being in whatever they are doing.

Willingness is a key factor in one's state of being. If I am unwilling to do what there is to do, that unwillingness shows up in my attitude, particularly in my emotional well-being. People do a lot of things unwillingly. Many people go to work every day because they "have to," not because they want to or even because they are willing to. They do it with a resistant attitude that shows up in many ways, including some "wear and tear" on their physical, emotional, and mental bodies. How I am "being" at any given time in my life is determined by the attitude that I choose to have at that given time.

Eli: Being able to choose how we are being is one of the most valuable skills of emotional intelligence. It requires an awareness of our capacity to let go of being *against* something, and replace it with being *for* something.

In other words, the question is, how can I be *for* life right now when life is not so easy to be *for*?

John: Exactly. When I can seriously ask that question and actually know that I have a real choice with which to answer, then it becomes obvious that my attitude and my feelings are not welded to the situation that life is presenting to me. That situation did not cause my resistance or my attitude or my level of willingness. I caused it. When that becomes absolutely clear to me, I am then in a position to shift from my automatic mind's reaction to a more spacious, clear mind-place that exists at a higher realm of functioning.

Eli: So, John, lets get back to the polarity of being versus doing. You said that you use your white board to write "Being" on the left side and "Doing" on the right. Illustrate that for me.

John: OK. I draw a horizontal line across the board under the words "Being" and "Doing" to make the chart below:

BEING	DOING
Present	Future
Experience	Success
Whole, complete	Results driven
Enough as is	More, progress

Then, to further elaborate, I draw a horizontal line across the board under those words and add two vertical lines so that the board looks like this:

Doing versus Being

	State of Being	State of Doing
Nature of State	Experience only "NOW" Fully present in body and senses.	Achieve goals Accomplishments Future oriented
Purpose of State	To grow *deeper*. To see reality as it is. To be fully connected to self and life.	Improve, Grow, Develop, Win, Make progress.
Beliefs in State	I'm content with myself. I am enough, open, strong, wise, caring.	I am good when I succeed, prove myself, do my best.
Feelings in State	Full range of feelings plus acceptance of self, others, and life.	Challenge, Pride, Pressure, Driven, Focused, Satisfaction, Excitement, Anxious

This figure depicts the states that exist at the two ends of the Being-Doing polarity. Whichever end of the polarity we focus on, our motivation follows. What we think about and how we see things follows wherever our attention is focused. Using this model, I ask my clients, "Where would you be at each of the ends of the polarity?" Typically they said, "The state of doing is at work; my state of being is at home or on vacation." Then,

Doing AND Being

	State of Being	State of Doing
Nature of State	Experience only "NOW" Fully present in body and senses.	Achieve goals Accomplishments Future oriented
Purpose of State	To grow *deeper*. To see reality as it is. To be fully connected to self and life.	Improve, Grow, Develop, Win, Make progress.
Beliefs in State	I'm content with myself I am enough, open, strong, wise, caring.	I am good when I succeed, prove myself, do my best.
Feelings in State	Full range of feelings plus acceptance of self, others, and life.	Challenge, Pride, Pressure, Driven, Focused, Satisfaction, Excitement, Anxious

. . . I would show the matrix above and ask what it would be like to remove the line that polarizes us between Doing and Being? What would have to shift?

Eli: . . . and they say?

John: At first they are puzzled. So I ask them to mentally see a picture of themselves at work having integrated both sides of themselves and to share with me what they created in their mind's eye. (This is an integration process done visually.)

Eli: I imagine many people in their work situations do not even consider blending such qualities of life as enjoyment, pleasure, satisfaction, or happiness into their work.

John: That's true. In his emotional intelligence workshops, Dr. Vergil Metts asks managers to guess what emotion is deemed most acceptable to be expressed in the American workplace. The correct answer according to the research is anger; if you are a male, being empathic, happy, caring, and sympathetic can be discounted in a heart beat. The emotions in the being side of us human beings seem to be stifled unless we are at home or on vacation.

Eli: So, what you want people to see is that they don't have to wait until they go home or on vacation to feel good. They could actually look forward to having good feelings at work if they so choose.

John: That's the point. It's a choice.

Eli: One way to facilitate a choice is to have the individual role play a dialogue between their two sides in order to get to the crux of their internal conflict.

John: Yes, in Gestalt work that's the paradox of achieving integration through exaggerating the separation. It's essentially thesis and antithesis coming together as a synthesis.

Eli: This synthesis is essentially the integration of the different sides of their conflict. From this new stance new perspectives typically develop.

John: In summary, when we have internal conflict we are a "house divided." By going through a process of integration we return to wholeness, to balance, and to the truth of our being.

Me and my shadow

Eli Mitchell & John Hoover

Eli: John, do you remember the vintage mystery radio show called *The Shadow*?

John: Oh yeah, it begins with, "Who knows what evil lurks in the hearts of men? Only the Shadow knows!"

Eli: That is so true, isn't it, John? The shadow part of our personality "knows," even if we don't admit it consciously. To paraphrase the poet Robert Frost, we are all, to some degree, acquainted with the night.

John: We sure are. As I understand it, in Jungian psychology the shadow is a repressed part of our psyche, our total personality, that we do not want to recognize or accept. According to Jung's early formulation, the shadow contains material that we find unacceptable, characteristics we abhor, and negatives we deny as our own.

Eli: Yes, and the term "shadow" typically conjures up dark images. However, it is not necessarily evil or even pejorative. Our shadow side is the aspect of ourselves that we disown, negative or positive. It can embody our denied "gold" (as Jung said), our unclaimed generosity, goodness, even saintliness. The shadow can be full of light.

True story: a therapist was leading a Hell's Angel type of biker through a guided imagery process to get him in touch with his deeper self. The image that popped-up for the biker was a radiantly white angel! This unacknowledged part (his shadow) was quite unnerving to him, representing what was opposite to his dark persona, or mask, that he showed the world.

John: It's understandable isn't it? The last thing in the world that guy wants to be seen as is caring, angelic, pure, and safe. He's spent a lot of his life making sure no one would see him as anything but mean, tough, and nasty! You know, Eli, I suspect that any extreme persona is an overcompensating ego hiding its opposite nature under that unconscious façade. Pretty creative, huh?

Eli: Yes, sir. Jung actually spoke of the shadow as "the seat of creativity." The infamous story, "Dr. Jekyll and Mr. Hyde," was dreamed-up (literally) by Robert Louis Stevenson; the obvious source was his shadow-side showing up in a nightmare.

John: The shadow, then, can contain generous deposits of "gold" and boundless creativity as well as demonic darkness—our evil nature, including cruelty, greed, and hideous violence. The Jungian explanation for terrible phenomena like the holocaust is that groups of people project their shadow onto others who are in some way different and thereby become scapegoats.

Eli: And on the flip side of being capable of mass murder, we humans have the capacity to sacrifice our lives to save others' lives.

John: So true. And the challenging psychological work for us is to "own" our shadow and deal with it so that our psyche will be more balanced. A Jungian saying is "the brighter the light, the longer the shadow." The shadow's energy, if run from, can erupt with a vengeance; take for example the pious TV evangelist who is caught with a prostitute.

Robert Johnson's book, *Owning Your Own Shadow,* discusses the problematical dynamics that occur when a repressed shadow is projected onto others.

Eli: I remember encountering a mild shadow projection of my own during an experiential workshop some years ago. At the check-in desk I met another participant who appeared to be a "bumbler," a seemingly inept person; I instantly disliked him and wanted to get away from him. As the workshop progressed, I realized my initial judgmental take was in error—this colleague was an astute professional. Turns out his negative impression on me was actually my projected shadow. My father was ineffective in some ways, and I have fears of being too much like him. Hence, I projected an aspect of my shadow onto this workshop associate because he originally personified some of my disowned characteristics.

John: Yeah, and that can sure catch us by surprise. One time I was talking with some friends about my disapproval of certain characteristics in my children. My friends laughed and said those traits were just like mine. When I heard that I felt myself becoming angry, confused, and embarrassed. I hated hearing that. How dare they say that about me! I felt my face getting hot, and I knew that must have meant I was guilty as charged!

Eli: Another shadow dynamic is, that since it resides in our unconscious, we occasionally can freak ourselves out with something that our minds dream up . . . literally.

John: Sounds like you'd like to recount a nightmare.

Eli: Yes. Once upon a time, as a graduate student, I was teaching a couple of courses to about seventy undergraduate students. I was being a "nice professor" and attempted to take care of the many (some invalid) requests from these students. I was assaulted with their appeals: "Can I drop this course, add this course, audit this course, change this course?" and so on. I made sweet, accommodating replies to all these appeals.

Some years earlier I had seen the scary (to me) movie *The Exorcist*. One night, following those first few days of classes, I had an "exorcism" nightmare.

A priest and I are standing at the bedside of a man who is obviously possessed. His bed is shaking violently, his head is spinning around, and he is vomiting vile material. As the priest is trying to perform an exorcism on this outraged figure, I'm standing there helpless and terrified.

When I abruptly wake-up my heart is pounding, and I am astounded at how perturbed I am from this dream.

Later that morning I decided to work on the dream in a Gestalt manner, that is, play the role of the different figures in the dream to see which dynamics I resonated with the most. When I played myself in the dream, I didn't feel much different than I actually felt in the dream. When I played the role of the priest, there was not much energy in that figure either. Then I laid on the floor and got into the role of the "possessed." Wow! Rage-full energy filled my body. ANGER. I was full of anger. I ranted and raved for awhile and then, exhausted, began to process what all that rage was about.

I realized that it was a shadow/compensation dream wherein my repressed shadow anger was expressed in an exaggerated manner. My dramatic rage expressed in the dream was compensation for my sugary persona that I had been living out, especially in relationship to my students.

John: So you got a good handle on what the nightmare was about. As you know, dreams not only can give us great insight into ourselves, they can also imply actions that would be in our best interest to take. What did you do with that dream?

Eli: I embraced my shadow rage and became much more assertive (not aggressive) in my interactions with others. When students came with more unreasonable requests, I firmly turned them down. These acts of assertiveness were freeing because I was no longer giving away my power to please others by doing for them what they could do for themselves.

John: So you acknowledged your shadow-side, accepted it, and handled your rage by transforming that energy into assertiveness.

17

Eli: Yes. Due to years of training in Gestalt therapy I was fortunate in that my modus operandi came relatively easy.

When writing about the shadow archetype, Jung gave fair warning that no "technique" could effectively deal with the shadow and that typically "long and difficult negotiations will be unavoidable."

John: So there are several courses of action—ways to negotiate—that can be employed to attend to our shadow dilemmas; the bottom line appears to be: the only way out is through.

Taming the inner critic

John Hoover

Have you ever wondered how to tame your inner critic? You know, the voice in your head that tells you you're not good enough, that your body should look like those in the outdoor or fashion magazines, that life always lets you down. Well, I have spent a lot of time wrestling with that incessant chatterbox throughout my life.

As I walk down my road of life, step by step, moment by moment, *life* is happening. What I'm referring to as *life* are all the situations, and events, and circumstances taking place in each and every moment.

Since my earliest beginning, at each step on my life's journey I have been doing something, thinking something, feeling something. While this is going on, imagine there is a movie camera in my head, and it is recording each and every moment. Everything that I see, hear, feel, think, do, or don't do is captured frame after frame.

Imagine the film of this movie as it passes on through the camera to a giant take up reel behind me. There I am, my entire past, frame after frame. However, as each frame passes through the camera, a judge evaluates everything I said, did, thought, felt, or, didn't say, didn't think, didn't do, and so forth. Each moment of me is graded on the judge's evaluative scale. In some instances the judge quickly decides that my thoughts, actions, or feelings were unacceptable, so an X is stamped across that frame of the movie.

Next, imagine the film goes on through the cutting room where all of the X-ed out frames are cut out of the film so that only the "approved" John Hoovers make it on to the giant take-up reel. Those X-ed out John Hoovers are excommunicated, and land on the cutting room floor. So if one looks at the take-up reel they will see many holes in the film that represent all of the X-ed out John Hoovers. Only the public, acceptable, edited John Hoovers make it to the reel.

But all of the excommunicated John Hoovers on the cutting room floor were real. I actually thought those things, said those things, felt those things, did those things, for real. But they are the times when John Hoover was judged "unacceptable." They became the secret, hidden, suppressed, and repressed aspects of myself which I then "disowned," so to speak.

Now visualize this picture. Imagine a freezing cold winter's night. But sitting comfortably and respectably in a cozy living room with a warm fire in the fireplace is the "sanitized," acceptable, public John Hoover. Outside in the howling wind in snow-covered night, shivers all of those excommunicated John Hoovers hauntingly peering into the windows and seeing the "good" John Hoover being warmed by the fire while they are all being ignored.

Until all of the disowned John Hoovers are reclaimed, there can be little wholeness in John Hoover's life. Since wholeness and health are derived from the same root word, in order for me to be of healthy mind, body, and spirit, I must attain wholeness. In this ideal state, I am fully who I am.

What's more, when the critic stamps that X on the movie frame he adds his own judgmental commentary to that moment, judgments like:

What an idiot I am.

I am such a looser.

She/he doesn't like me.

I've really screwed up; I am just a phony.

I'm incompetent.

I'm stupid.

I'm no good.

This inner critic, which Dr. Lewis Paul called the "Inner Cruel Critic" and Dr. Bradford Brown called the "Crafty Little Sucker," turns out to be the most harmful aspect of the human experience.

When my very own inner critic judged me for a certain behavior, it was easy for me to believe that I had transgressed or done something wrong. Thus I wanted to hide my transgression in order to escape punishment for my wrongdoing and the accompanying negative feelings of shame and guilt. In doing so, I disowned that segment of my behavior as if it were not me.

"I didn't do anything; It wasn't my fault; I'm innocent." So I try to hide the part of me that behaved in that manner, and I artificially split myself into two false selves: the "good" one and the "bad" one.

There are, of course, ways to deal with one's inner critic. Here's an example of how I typically handle its running commentary.

I wake up in the morning, look over at the alarm clock, and see that I'm late for my first appointment with a client. I feel a surprise shock, and I jump out of bed muttering something about the alarm. "How could I forget?" "Who am I supposed to be seeing right now?" "Damn . . . gotta brush my teeth."

I throw on my clothes and rush off to my appointment arriving a half-hour late, feeling frenzied, anxious, guilty, embarrassed, and apologetic toward my client. I feel out of sorts pretty much all day.

Near the end of the work day I had a client cancellation so I did a process I have practiced in the More to Life Program that is similar to a number of other cognitive therapy models.

First, I closed my eyes and went back in time to the moment I felt that shock while looking at my alarm clock, and I put my hand on my body where I felt the shock.

By re-experiencing that moment and allowing myself to feel that same shock (albeit less powerfully than the first time) and just focusing my attention on the feeling, I could then become aware of what my unconscious and automatic mind had made up earlier that morning.

Next, I then wrote down the unconscious thoughts that were there in my head in that half-second period of time when I felt that shock. I would notice a couple thoughts, write them on the board, then go back to the shock moment again and notice a couple more thoughts. I'd write them down and keep doing that until the thoughts were finished. At the end of this part of the process, the board looked something like this:

Oh no. I've overslept.

That can't be.

I have blown it.

I forgot to set the alarm.

This is terrible.

I can't even set the alarm right.

I am losing it.

I'm getting senile.

I have Alzheimer's.

Whoever I'm supposed to be seeing will be pissed.

I'm a fool.

I am unprofessional.

I am a phony.

I am a fake.

I am a nothing.

It's all going to come out that I am incompetent.

I should quit.

Then, continuing to use the More to Life process, I looked at each statement and determined if it was: true, false, or don't know. The crucible here is that in order for a statement to be considered true:

- It must be objectively verifiable, that is it must have existence in reality.
- It can't be a judgment, opinion, or prediction—they exist only in one's mind.
- All feelings are experienced—and are true.
- Beliefs do not exist in reality, but in our minds. We can have beliefs about reality but the beliefs themselves are not in and of themselves real.

When I verified the statements, only two were true: "I've overslept," and "I forgot to set the alarm." The rest were false.

The process of addressing each statement and declaring it to be true, false, or don't know is the method of clearing false beliefs and releasing ourselves from the negative feelings that we had.

It is easy for us to think the events cause our feelings. In the More to Life program they call that "false cause," because the actual event didn't make me feel negative; my negative feelings were the result of the judgments and predictions created by my reactive inner critic.

Once I'd told the truth about what had happened and disposed of the lies my mind had been telling me, I was freed from them, I felt more whole, and I could readily choose how I wished to proceed with my life.

Play therapy

Eli Mitchell

Last spring sitting on my back deck working on this book, I noticed several birds frolicking around a small statue of St. Francis of Assisi. This solemn patron saint of animals stands amid my backyard forsythia and looks down at an adoring bird perched in the palm of his hand. It was comical to watch a cardinal, a chickadee, and then a tufted titmouse take turns perching on St. Francis' seriously hooded head.

This spirited scene reminded me that sometimes our psychotherapy can really be play therapy. That is, a "work situation" or problem can sometimes be turned into a fun experience, and the job gets done or the problem solved positively.

Here's a therapeutic play story about undoing an antagonistic upward spiral. Early in our marriage Lucy would typically get up earlier than I did and sometimes would be annoyed by my "sleeping-in." One morning when I was slow on the uptake Lucy mused that sometime she might throw water on me to get me going. I knew immediately that would push a big negative button of mine and, I would be infuriated. I firmly warned Lucy, "Don't do that one; I just might lose it."

One morning, some weeks later, we had an insignificant disagreement, and as I was heading out of the house for a jog in the neighborhood Lucy splashed my chest with a partial glass of water. I stuffed my instant rage, exited the house, and escalated my jog into an intense hundred yard dash chanting, "No, no," the whole time. My fury thereby being reduced to anger and then to irritation, I huffed and puffed and loped along and thought about what to do that would be the *opposite* of what my angry thoughts called for. And that was go home and get into a shouting match with Lucy.

Suddenly it occurred to me that I could be playful rather than reacting to Lucy's action. When I got to the house I jumped in the car, drove to the drug store, and bought a couple of water pistols. Returning home I filled them with water, found Lucy, tossed her a gun, and then fired the first volley. She immediately returned fire. After soaking each other we fell into a wet, hugging heap, laughing all the way. Lucy and I are bemused when we recall this soggy skirmish, since we have no idea what caused this tiff in the first place.

By the way, Lucy has never thrown water on me again.

How and why to effectively say "NO"

John Hoover & Eli Mitchell

Eli: John, do you notice how our clients struggle with saying "no" while infants can't not?

John: Absolutely! Infants don't have words but they do have sounds with considerable volume. They may not be able to verbalize "I'm very upset" or "I'm really hungry" or "Can't you see I've got a freaking rash!" So, they cry loudly. They get their feelings out.

Eli: They hold nothing back.

John: Their message is saying "no" to the circumstances they find themselves in. They cry and scream, indicating "I don't like this one bit! I hate this! No, no, no!"

Eli: So, what happens between infancy and adulthood that causes us to undermine our very selves?

John: The bottom line is this. When children learn that it is not OK to vocally object to their circumstances, they may learn that it isn't OK to express their feelings and preferences at all.

Eli: So the older child's screams elicit disapproval, scolding, or withheld love from parents. That's powerful stuff. But in the beginning, the infant doesn't hoove the prerequisite skills to do otherwise. He's born with the survival crying and screaming instinct.

John: That whole stage from early survival instinct to polite social conduct is very fundamental in the development of self expression. The growing child, like all animals, cues into parents' behaviors, attitudes, pleasures, and displeasures. They are learning to be a human animal.

Eli: As I see it, there's a delicate balance going on between some parents' heavy-handed disapproval of a how a child expresses wants, needs, and demands, on one hand, and the total absence of appropriate limits on the child, on the other hand.

John: If a child has insufficient limits placed on him from his parents, he may grow up with a sense of entitlement, expecting life to always meet his demands and desires . . . in other words, he typically turns into a "spoiled individual."

If parents are overly controlling and disapproving of the child's assertions, which are simply the child's expressions of wanting to establish his place in the world, the child may try to thwart his own impulses, wants, needs, and desires.

Eli: In other words, that child's self-expression becomes contained, withheld, suppressed . . . pushed to the "shadow side" of the unconscious mind.

John: Yes, and that's exactly what I did . . . with a little help from my folks. My picture of that process looks something like this: Every child comes into this world with their little list of preferences.

Eli: What do you mean list?

John: I mean those few preferences that an infant has from the time they were born. Why does one infant like to be held in a certain way and another infant doesn't like to be held that way? Why does one child like Gerber's puréed pears but doesn't like Gerber's puréed peaches? And another infant likes just the opposite?

Eli: They just do.

John: Yeah, it's just their preference. It's who they are, so to speak. It came with the kid . . . a little preference list. But first off, the child encounters an environment of parents who happen to also have a list of preferences. It's a big list and it includes their preferences for how they want their child to be! For example, ever see those day-old babies sitting in their little bassinets on display in the hospital labor and delivery wing? Fathers and friends can look through the window and see the newbies. Imagine somebody walks in behind those babies and claps their hands together loudly. You might see one baby begin screaming, his face turning bright red, and his arms and legs go thrashing out and shaking. Maybe the one next to the screaming baby doesn't change expressions at all. Maybe another one frowns, and another one looks around alertly, and another one starts making bubbles, or whatever.

So forty years later we go to where each of those babies is working and inquire about them. Let's say that first baby's name is Fred. We ask the people where he works to tell us about Fred. They say, "Oh, Fred is just so thin-skinned; everything bothers him; he's so sensitive, gets upset real easily." We find the next baby's place of employment and ask about Roger. They say something like: Oh, you mean Buddha? He's just so laid-back, easy-going; nothing upsets him, he just goes at his own pace.

You get the picture? This refers to what I think of as an energy package that comes with every one of us at birth, and stays with us throughout our life.

Eli: I think that is what we call our basic temperament. That is part of the psyche's structure. We see a distinctive personality component showing up in children from day one.

John: So that "energy package" from day one, also includes inherent preferences for certain things in life, just because it's who they are. But when parents' preferences for how they want their child to be differs from who the child is, well, there's the rub.

The parents' preferences for how they want their child to be are like a picture of their ideal child that they have in their mind. It's like that mind-picture is then held up in front of their actual child. When their child doesn't match their picture they are likely to show disappointment and disapproval. They are more attached to their idealized version of their child than to their actual child, and they miss out on having an authentic relationship with their real child. In a sense they don't want to really see the child as he/she really is. For example, before my first child was born, I had a preference for what kind of a kid I wanted him to be.

Eli: And your kid wasn't even a him!

John: That's right. Karin Suzanne surprised us with her gender! A parent's preference for the child's gender is common. Since the advent of the sonogram parents today generally have several months to psychologically prepare to meet their baby boy or girl. I have heard many clients tell me that their parents wanted the other gender than the one they are. They talk about it as if that preference remains in perpetuity, and therefore they can never live up to that expectation. I think many children believe that they must try to live up to all of their parents' preferences and expectations, fearing that somehow they are a disappointment if they don't.

Eli: Then what can happen is that the child tries to thwart their natural patterns and preferences in order to match their parents' picture. When that happens, the child trades off getting acceptance for getting approval.

John: That's right, because acceptance is about who you are, whereas approval is about what you do! So children begin doing things in certain ways in order to get approval; they don't want to risk being rejected when they act spontaneously and naturally. Which is what is necessary in order to be who you are. So those children try to prefer only those things that are acceptable to the parents, particularly if the parents make it their business to control the children's interests, choices, inclinations.

Eli: When children become completely "socialized" into performing their lives strictly according to the parents' preferences it can make it difficult for the child to get in touch with his authentic self, where his preferences, needs, and comforts reside. He wouldn't be able to truly answer the question: "What do you want?" He would be automatically screening out what he wants in order to answer the question in a way that would please whoever was asking the question. And, I believe every child goes through some degree of this.

John: Yes, right up to that age at which "raging hormones" kick in and that adolescent surge takes over. I can still remember the time my wife, Sharon said to our youngest daughter, Elizabeth: "Who are you and what have you done with Elizabeth!"

Eli: I suspect the more "socialized" and compliant the child is required to be, the more severe or abrupt the changes come out during adolescence.

John: For some, changing patterns to become more individuated in adolescence is rough. I was too scared of my father to challenge his authority. So I became outwardly compliant, but inwardly defiant. I was well schooled to become a passive-aggressive adult, though I did go through a phase of being outwardly defiant shortly after leaving home.

All that we're talking about here, Eli, has to do with that act of saying "NO!" That "no process" that we had folks do in our Gestalt groups represented the zillions of times that a person felt like saying no, but acquiesced to going along with what somebody else wanted, required, demanded, begged, or whatever that caused the child to feel obliged to do. And when the child did it, he knew that it somehow diminished his own sense of self. It wasn't his preference. It was the other person's preference. He hadn't really chosen it.

Eli: That's where the "I prefer not" phrase comes into play isn't it?

John: Yes. In the Assertiveness Training program we teach people to use the phrase "I prefer not" to represent standing up for oneself. We teach them that you don't have to make up excuses or lie to someone who is making a request of you to which you don't really want to comply. No excuse has one cubit of true power in it. One of the most powerful things you can do is to say something that represents who you are fundamentally. Your preferences are that; they represent you in that very moment.

Eli: Give an example of that, John.

John: Suppose somebody asks to borrow your car. For whatever reason, you don't feel comfortable lending it to that person. So you make up some excuse like: it's not running well, or, I don't have insurance that covers anybody else driving it, or, my daughter needs it, et cetera. Since they are all excuses, they are all lies. The real truth is you don't prefer lending your car. The most powerful thing you can say is: "I prefer not lending my car."

If you make an excuse like "I don't have insurance," they may counter with: "That's OK, I have insurance that covers any vehicle I drive." If you say your car is not running well, they might say: "That's OK, if it messes up my brother will be with me, and he's a top notch mechanic." And on it goes. But if you say, "I prefer not lending my vehicle," what can they say? All they can do is ask why not? And that means they want you to give some excuse that they can quite easily counter. But when your reply is: "Because that's my preference," it is a statement that is based in your personhood, in your perfect right to say "yes" or "no" simply because you are a human being that makes choices and has preferences of your own making.

Eli: That is quite simply an elegant way of saying "no" and indeed a practice of standing in your own authority. But, what if they counter with, "I thought you were my friend."

John: "Sounds like you believe that if I don't let you use my car I am not a friend. But that's not true. I am a friend, *and* I have a personal preference to not lend my car to anybody."

Eli: So when people haven't stepped into their own authority, they are missing that they have a perfect right to feel what they feel, and to prefer what they prefer.

John: This way of forming boundaries allows all of us to have the freedom of choice to say "yes" or to say "no" to the requests that other people make of us. Boundaries are made up of words. And the most powerful boundary words turn out to be "no" and "I prefer not."

Protecting our children from the tsunami

Eli Mitchell

Our children need protection not only from day-to-day hazards, harmful acts of nature, or predatory and/or careless people, but also from the never-ending media tsunami. Since our Western culture is a culture of sex and violence, it is of primary importance that parents and other caregivers provide children with the feeling of being guarded and safe.

Kids are easily traumatized by media violence, adult sexual scenes, and scary stories. They can be suddenly overwhelmed by X-rated scenes or even "soft" porn. And, like us grown-ups, children can be surely spooked by violent and/or horror movies. Also, like us adults, nightmares kindled by the media can be very unsettling to our kids. Parents do well by their children to hear-out disturbing dreams (even in the middle of the night) and to offer reassurance.

What follows is a family therapy narrative, a ghost story in fact, related to issues of protection and support.

Matthew and Susan, parents of twelve-year-old Nate, came into family therapy with the presenting problem that Nate had stubbornly refused to sleep alone in his bedroom for the past three years. Whenever he went to bed alone, Nate was constantly afraid and unable to go to sleep. The only way that this situation was resolved was that Nate's mother slept beside him in his bed which was pushed against a wall. Then he was able to get a good night rest by sleeping between his mother and the bedroom wall. It's notable that Nate confided in me that he actually detested this sleeping arrangement, but nobody had come up with a better solution.

When I took a family history over several initial sessions, two main dynamics stood out. First, Matthew, a moderately successful attorney, evidently was born with a temperament which tended toward anxiousness. His life history was filled with episodes of being over-anxious and easily embarrassed. He had been on psychotropic medication for years to help him deal with a generalized anxiety disorder.

Since research tells us that temperament can be inherited, I figured that Nate could possibly have a genetic tendency toward above-normal levels of anxiety.

Secondly, and more pertinent to Nate's fears of sleeping alone, were his early-in-life experiences. For several months after his birth,

Nate's pediatrician labeled him as a "failure to thrive" infant. That's the condition when an infant is unable to receive sufficient nutrition, doesn't gain weight, and therefore does not grow physically.

In Nate's case, at three months old he was diagnosed with gastroesophageal reflux (GER). Also, for the first four years of his life he was plagued with sleep apnea. Because of these physiological difficulties, for his survival his mother found it necessary to sleep beside Nate for these four years. He overcame these problems to the extent that he was able to sleep alone in his own bed for the next five years.

Inexplicable to his parents, one summer night when Nate was nine years-old he became terrified with the prospect of sleeping alone. Matthew and Susan's ultimate solution to deal with Nate's development of extreme night fright turned out to be for his mother to sleep in Nate's bed with him.

This is where the "ghost story" starts.

When Nate was nine his family went on a summer vacation to Charleston, South Carolina. One evening the whole family took a tour of the ghost haunts of this pre-revolutionary war city. The group toured several sites where ghosts supposedly "hung out" (literally and figuratively), and they spent some time at an eighteenth-century graveyard. The tour guide even presented photographs of ghosts hovering over these graves. Evidently this unnerving experience convinced Nate that ghosts were not a fiction but a reality.

That was the beginning of his fear of the dark and not-sleeping-alone problems. When Nate later demanded his mother sleep beside him, he had regressed to that time of great comfort at night during the first four years of his life.

The plot thickens. A year or so after the ghost tour episode, Nate was visiting a friend whose teenage siblings were watching a horror movie "The Ring." Even though Nate and friend only watched the first part of this movie, Nate's belief in ghosts was reinforced, and his insecurities of being in the dark and sleeping alone were heightened.

When he was twelve, Nate's introduction to another product of horror media, the video game "Staying Alive," was the last straw. Nate's escalated fears precipitated his parents initiating family psychotherapy with me. After we tried different ways to help him overcome his anxieties, and thereby be able to sleep alone again (with no success), Nate's parents and I decided on a behavioral solution. We asked him to decide on something he would really like to earn. Nate concluded that the item he would work the hardest for would be his very own cell phone. Matthew, Susan, Nate, and I developed and signed the following contract:

We parents agree to reward you $20.00 each night in a row sleeping alone successfully. Anything (within reason) can be used to aide in sleeping alone, such as TV, extra pillows, and the overhead light turned on. The money earned is to be used exclusively toward the purchase of a cell phone. There will be a $10.00 deduction for each night that you, Nate, fail to sleep alone. The day after the final reward of enough money to buy a cell phone, we will take you to the store in order for you to purchase one.

Determined to succeed, Nate pushed through his fears and kept this contract to the letter.

Evidently the motivation to own his own cell phone trumped his terror of sleeping alone. To his and her relief, Nate's mother did not have to sleep beside him anymore.

There was one glitch, however. In the contract we did not specify a monetary limit to the cost of the cell phone. Nate held out for a state-of-the-art phone that cost hundreds of dollars. When, with chagrin, I discussed this unanticipated expense with Dad he was very gracious and said, "Not a problem, Doc, it's worth it."

Would you prefer to be gratified or satisfied?

John Hoover

In a psychology workshop in Knoxville, I remember the trainer asking the group, "How many of you work with families?" One of my most delightful colleagues, Pauline Eastham, Ph.D., answered, "When I work with individuals I am always working with families whether or not they are actually present in the room!" That reminded me that in the same way, I think whatever relationships are being worked on in therapy, there is always the relationship with oneself to work through.

There is a model that my friend David Hoffman, Ph.D., shared with me years ago that I refer to as The Hoffman Satisfaction-Gratification model. David identifies a certain dynamic that is inherent in *satisfaction* that is not inherent in *gratification*. Dr. Hoffman believes that it is important to undo the confusion between them because many people hear gratification and satisfaction as synonymous. But Dr. Hoffman states: "Gratifiers don't satisfy, they do gratify. Satisfaction is something else . . . a successful relationship with the self."

In addition to his private practice of psychology in Phoenix, Arizona, David Hoffman, Ph.D. has worked as a consultant and trainer with a number of major corporations in the United States. He developed a process for working with managers who were responsible for motivating their subordinates to accomplish their work objectives.

David's training usually took place in a corporate room with maybe 35 managers or supervisors. One focus of this particular workshop was on understanding motivation. What is motivation? Where does it come from? How do we evoke it? How do we bring it out of our people?

The supervisors discussed the questions in small groups and generally concluded that in order to motivate people you have to start with something that inspires rather than scares people. They concluded that people should be inspired by providing some kind of rewards that everybody would like or value or appreciate. Something that makes people feel good.

Listing their ideas on the board, they brainstormed everything they could think of that might make people feel good. The list included: bonuses, recognition, employee of the month, special parking space for the month, raises, time off, "at-a-boy" announcements in the news letter, and so on. They even brainstormed not so serious things like sex, booze, back rubs, and cigar breaks, with the justification that those things can make you feel good. They also came up with other such feel-good things as: special T-shirts, badges, banners in the hallway, finishing the work ahead of schedule, getting to leave work early, getting to come to work late, as well as breaking the production record or doing a really good job.

On the board David put a line vertically separating the 28 ideas on the left hand side from the two or three brainstorming ideas on the right-hand side. On the right side of the board were: doing a really good job, breaking the production record, and finishing the work ahead of schedule.

The process that followed was something like this. Looking at everything on the left side of the board David wrote the heading "Gratification." On the right side he wrote the heading "Satisfaction."

David then pointed out some common denominators of the items under the heading of "Gratification:"

1. These are feel-good things or activities (motivator items) that come from others (outside of the person) and given to the person. Examples include money, booze, tickets to a game, prizes, awards, bonuses, recognition, gifts, food, et cetera.

2. There is a limit to the amount of "motivator items" that can reasonably be given. For example there are not unlimited bonuses, prizes, or awards that can be doled out.

3. Gratifiers lose their ability to gratify. For example the length of time an employee feels motivated from receiving a bonus, prizes, or other recognition is reported to be short-lived.

4. Gratifiers elicit a kind of "addiction pattern." Whatever amount of the gratifier that motivated people the first time will not be enough to motivate them the second time; it would take more of that same gratifier to have an equivalent impact.

5. Over time, gratifiers can actually become disincentives. For example, if employees receive the same bonus this year as they got last year they might grumble, believing that they should have gotten more. And if there is no bonus to give, it can be seen as a de-motivator because the workers come to expect the bonus.

On the right side of the board was written: "Satisfaction." The distinction of a satisfier is that it comes from one's self, to themselves, for themselves.

1. These are feel-good things that come from inside the individual worker.

2. The source of satisfaction therefore is unlimited. You would never run out of the supply.

3. Satisfaction creates a positive impact that does not diminish regardless of how many times it is used.

4. Satisfaction does not depend on anyone else.

5. Satisfaction engenders a positive relationship with your self .

The strength behind the satisfaction side exists because it forms a successful relationship with the self. Dr. Hoffman stated, "It is important to clarify that there is nothing wrong with gratifiers. They give us pleasure. Gratifiers meet some of our needs very nicely. The confusion is . . . seeking satisfaction by accumulating gratifiers—and it doesn't work. You might get *satiation,* but not satisfaction. If you want gratification, go for the gratifiers, and enjoy; but you won't get satisfaction. If you want satisfaction, there is a simple formula made up of three components that leads to a successful relationship with the self." He wrote those components on the board as follows:

1. Keep your agreements.

2. Press your limits.

3. Do your best.

Keep your agreements means: say what you're going to do and do what you say. When we decide on a goal that we choose for ourselves, we are making a commitment to do something. If we make a commitment to do something and don't do it, who is it that always knows that we didn't do it? WE always know. Notice then, what kind of a relationship do we have with our self—successful or unsuccessful? High or low self-regard? . . . self-esteem? . . . self-worth? . . . self-confidence?

When you make an agreement (with yourself) to do something challenging, and you do what you said, there is a certain feeling inside of you that comes in no other way. You feel something about yourself that can only come from you. You stand up straighter, walk with more dignity, feel grounded, self-reliant, and calm because it represents a successful relationship with the self inside of you. And every time we create such an experience, our entire "self system" is empowered. The "feel good" experience from giving your word and keeping it in the face of a challenge is distinctive, unique, and definitely different from the gratification type of "feel good."

The second component of the satisfaction formula is: **Press your limits**. Notice when you hear yourself thinking thoughts like, "I can't do this," "It's too hard," or "It won't work." Those are limiting thoughts, and if you don't challenge them or press against them they will limit you. It boils down to this. When we stop pressing our limits, we stop growing. Our vitality, curiosity, and expansion drops. I think everybody knows some old people who may be wrinkled but they aren't old because there is vitality in them; they're still interested in learning more. At the same time we all know people who haven't grown since their high school prom!

When we press our limits, we become more of ourselves than we were before. We discover more of our potential that has always been inside, waiting to be "pressed into service," that we wouldn't have found if we stopped wanting to grow.

Do your best is the third component of the formula. You always know when you've given some task your best shot and when you haven't. Doing your best is not a competition to better some "high-water mark" that you or someone else attained.

Dr. Hoffman said that the most important feature of doing your best is the resulting expansion of your whole sense of self and what is in your power to do. He said it is about how it makes you feel to acknowledge yourself for being intentional, focused, and present in whatever task you are doing.

Here is a story Dr. Hoffman shared about working with a college student who was a very depressed (dysphoric, dysthymic) person. One day she said, "We've got to hurry; I'm going to graduate in six months." Dr. Hoffman told her that if she would walk around the block where she lived everyday for two weeks, then he would walk with her (so she would have a support partner for the walking). Both the student and Dr Hoffman kept their agreements. They went to the track around the football field at Illinois State University and walked four times around—one mile. (Doing their best). After a couple weeks they would walk one, run one, walk one, run one. (Doing their best)

After a couple more weeks they would walk one, run two, walk one. (Doing their best) After a couple more weeks they would run three, walk one. (Doing their best). Then they began running four times around the track. Doing their best had grown dramatically. After a few more weeks, they began running in the streets about two miles (Doing their best—still expanding). Then they ran a 5K race, and later a 10K. They kept their agreements, and they pressed their limits. Hoffman said that it was not easy to show up some times. But they did their best and the growth was obvious at many levels.

Dr. Hoffman's student graduated depression-free. Some time later she wrote to Dr. Hoffman that she was off all medications, was a dedicated runner, and was doing 10Ks at her new location.

Dealing constructively with anger

John Hoover & Eli Mitchell

Eli: It's interesting to think about the stories that clients bring to the therapy room. Their stories are basically about unexpressed anger, fear, or sadness and they need help in getting through those feelings, particularly anger and the many forms that anger has.

John: I agree there are a lot of forms of anger as well as degrees of anger. Anger includes that whole range from slight annoyance to resentment to abject rage. It's all anger, but a little anger is quite different from enormous anger.

Eli: And depending on the intensity of anger, we use different words for it, like: irritated, frustrated, annoyed, hacked off, mad, furious, and enraged.

John: Regardless of the level of intensity, all anger is blame, from the slightest annoyance to the greatest rage. Behind all anger is a "position," a stand, so to speak, against something.

Eli: Our anger wants to strike back, control, or punish. One thing about anger is that it always needs a target; whether that target is people, or circumstances, or situations, or fate, or God. And, unexpressed anger is harmful and can lead to depression.

John: That's anger turned inward, and it's best not to direct anger at yourself, right?

Eli: Yes, it should be ex-pressed or pressed out. That means to press out the emotion from your body out into the universe. Of course that requires learning how to manage the delivery of that anger going out!

John: Since all anger is blame, let's talk about the process of blaming, in order to get a closer look at the blame game.

Eli: Well I know the blame game features the word "should," or "shouldn't" being applied to some action or situation that is disapproved of by the blamer.

John: Right. The interesting thing is that when we are blaming, we are rejecting some form of reality as it exists or might exist. For example, if I say (or even just think), "That driver in front of me is going too slow," I feel the impatience, and I may not even realize that I am blaming that driver. But I am, by believing that he should be going faster. The reality is that the driver is going at exactly the speed he is going. My "should" is a judgmental blame, as if that driver is required to comply with my idea of how fast he ought to be going.

Eli: If we split that word up—judge – mental—we have a mental judge inside fabricating a version of how I want reality to be. That means the blamer has an adversarial relationship with reality.

John: And since reality is going to win every time, we have a lot of experiences of being impatient in our lives when things aren't going exactly as we want them to go. To the baseball player that dropped the ball, I gasp, "He should have caught the ball." To my wife I say, "You should have called me before making plans for Friday evening." To the powers that be, I fume and fuss that they shouldn't have reacted to 9/11 the way they did. In reality the player didn't catch the ball, my wife didn't make the call, and they reacted to 9/11 the way they did. Neither the player, nor my wife, nor the powers that be, and certainly not my fabricated judgmental accusations can undo one cubit of reality. My "should" demand on reality is impossible to fulfill.

Eli: That's why we often feel so frustrated and angry. We are powerless to the reality of the truth of what has happened. Notice that powerlessness and helplessness is at the base of anger! In our discussion about rage we talk more about how violence is the most extreme form of powerlessness and helplessness. No one can undo what in fact did happen, no matter how much one dislikes what has transpired.

John: Yes, instead we need to embrace reality. We need to see reality clearly as it is, rather than resisting it, rejecting it, or obscuring it. When reality doesn't meet our preferred version, we can feel victimized. We may scream "NO, NO, NO, this can't be happening!" Our mind doesn't want to accept the reality that is, so it generates thoughts of being powerless. That's when we may react in anger, really believing we have been unfairly treated. We lash out at the source that we believe victimized us, be it a person, fate, circumstances, et cetera.

Eli: In a workshop on managing anger, the presenter commented: "When we are angry, we feel like a victim but we look like an abuser!" That really supports the idea that we feel powerless when we are angry. And unless you move on from that position, by accepting reality as it is and adjusting your intentions, you will continue to carry anger, as resentment, insisting on your mental version of how you wanted it to be, and in so doing, harm your own physical and emotional well-being.

John: I remember something a trainer in the More to Life program said one time, that resentment is like taking poison and expecting the other person to die. And that fits. I think of anger's energy as hot, alive, present, visible, enervating one's voice and expression. I think of resentment as moldy, old anger being carried around like a heavy stinky, gloomy, smoldering, pile of you-know-what!

Eli: No form of anger is pretty, but it doesn't have to be ugly either. I think the point here is that when anger arises in us, which it does quite frequently, we need to do something with that energy that is constructive rather than destructive.

John: And that includes the destructiveness of keeping it hidden inside as resentment, as well as the attacking form of anger in which we impulsively, aggressively abuse people.

Eli: On the constructive side, anger expressed effectively and assertively (rather than in an aggressive manner) can definitely lead to positive change. That whole model you have—For and Against—is a good one to describe the process of doing something constructive when we are stuck in a state of anger. Let's be sure to cover that model. But for now, we're focusing on the nature of anger itself being blame and criticism.

John: Yes, that is a very important notion to me. It helps me to be self aware. Whenever I can detect the feeling of any form of anger inside of me it becomes an undeniable signal that I am in the "blame game," believing that I know how something or someone *should* be.

Eli: And, furthermore, feeling a need to punish them, criticism them, scold them, blame them, or at least withhold loving kindness and compassion from them.

John: Yeah, wanting to hurt them to be exact.

Eli: So given that principle that "all feelings are meant to be expressed" what do you do?

John: Well, the first step is to remember the commitment to achieve an objective perspective on my subjective emotional experience. Then, from that perspective I can more easily dis-identify with the emotion. When we feel emotional, it's easy for us to identify ourselves as though *that* is who we are.

Eli: You mean, I may have an emotion, but I am not my emotion.

John: Yes. My emotion is not who I am.

Eli: So you identify more with the *awareness* of what's going on inside of you than the *feeling* of what's going on inside of you.

John: It seems that way to me. And the awareness includes what's going on outside of me as well, and also what's going on in my thinking mind. The mysterious "I" is sort of my state of being present in the moment, aware of my surroundings, my thinking, and my feelings. From that present-centered state, I can quite readily report out (express out to the universe) what I'm feeling, what I'm believing, and how I see the situation that I'm in.

Recently my friend David Howard stood up at a meeting of about 25 people. He said, "Folks, I've got to tell you I am mad as hell right now. I'm believing that none of y'all are on board with what needs to be done to keep this program alive. I know I'm blaming you, but that's how I see it right now, and I'm believing that you don't care enough about the program to take a little risk and enroll people in the best life-changing training they can possibly ever have in their lives!"

He then drew a couple of deep breaths and said, "Look, this program means everything to me, and I'm scared, really scared that we are going to let it just dry up and go away. We've just got to do something. I'm sorry for my outburst, but I'm not sorry for my passion."

Eli: Whew! Yeah, that's a good example. David felt anger and he owned it. He didn't say you made me angry, he said, "I am mad as hell." He owned that he was the source of the anger. And he said, "I am believing that none of you are on board," et cetera, and then said, "I know I'm blaming you," so he owned his belief and blame as well.

John: Yes, and after David owned his blame, he went on to say, "But that's how I'm seeing it right now." Notice he reveals the context of his perspective by saying, "That's how I'm seeing it." He isn't saying that's the way it is, but that's how he perceives it. He was owning that he had a point of view, a personal frame of reference.

Eli: And, when David added, "right now" he made it clear that his point of view was taking place in a frame of time . . . in the present. That's called his "emotional truth."

John: Say some more about the concept of emotional truth.

Eli: When someone is acutely aware of an intense feeling and they express themselves with forceful words, that is their emotional truth. Hank Williams' song, "I'm so lonesome, I could die" tells it all. Emotional truth is one's truth about what they are feeling in the moment. However, the "truth" could be very different later, once the emotion is expressed or subsides.

John: How so?

Eli: Let me give you an example from early in my marriage.

One time I was really angry with Lucy about something and yelled "I can't stand you, we're DONE. I never want to ever see you again!" Notice those words expressed how I felt at the moment, that is, my emotional truth. Lucy was able to accommodate or make room for my expressions of strong angry feelings, and consequently my emotional barometer was lowered. At this point we agreed on a "time out" and planned to meet again in three hours. Within an hour or so, I became aware of not only wanting to "stand" her and see her again, but I was eager to hear her out, to resolve our differences, and to move on.

John: So once you fully expressed your emotional truth, you soon were in touch with the real truth; you had emptied your anger and now you desired to get through your conflict and resume your loving relationship.

Eli: You got it. Emotional truth is momentary truth. Therefore, like David did, it's best to include in our feeling statements a "right now" in order to own that our negative emotion is temporary. To say, "Right now I don't like you!" is a much easier "truth" for our partner to handle than if we were to just say "I don't like you."

John: Yes, absolutely, Eli.

Eli: Here's another example of how one might handle anger. As a monetarily poor grad student at University of Tennessee Knoxville, over a period of three years I lived in two impoverished neighborhoods. Both of my apartments were broken into, and my personal stuff, as well as the meager amount of saleable items I owned (like a stereo or a TV) were stolen. After the first instance of being robbed, what hurt the most were feelings of violation and helplessness.

Also hurtful was my depression over the loss of memorabilia I treasured from my U.S. Navy travels: an African mask, a statue of Buddha, rare coins, and so on. Primarily, how I depressed myself was by stuffing my anger and, secondarily, by not expressing any sadness over my losses. For days following the first looting I was a downer guy . . . irritable, bitter, joyless, with nowhere to go with my resentment.

John: Ouch. That's a lot of pain to hold inside, Eli. And you said you were robbed twice. Did those feelings occur all over again after the second robbery too?

Eli: Glad you asked. No, it did not because of the "No Process" you taught me. Right after I discovered this thievery, I began to be consumed with negative feelings. However, as I was standing there in my apartment, surveying my losses, I decided to put the "No Process" into action: after picturing the robber on my (unstolen) sofa, I dropped to my knees, pounded "him" with my fists and shouted "no" with each blow until exhaustion, until I could barely raise my arms to strike anymore, until I lost my voice.

John: All right! Good going.

Eli: Thanks. The good news is I was not depressed. Instead, I was relieved. And my relief lasted; I wasn't consumed with unexpressed anger or bitterness, and my attitude about being deprived of "things" was much better.

John: Sounds like doing the "No Process" moved you through those unpleasant emotions and into some inner peace. Good for you. By the way, your positive attitude afterward reminds me of the saying, "The best things in life aren't things."

Owning one's uglies—Response-Ability

Eli Mitchell

Several months after my May 1977 marriage to Lucy, we went to a South Carolina beach for a few days. I invited my best hometown friend to join us so he could get to know Lucy better. The first day Jim was there they "got along famously." With a lot of poignancy and laughter they told each other their life stories. Also, all day the three of us rode waves, played in the sand, and that evening we dined on scrumptious Lowcountry seafood.

Later that night I became aware of the green-eyed monster's presence as I thought about how famously my bride and Jim had gotten along . . . too famously to suit me!

Fortunately, I had learned something in grad school and knew what there was to do—"own my uglies" with Lucy.

As we were hitting the sack I told Lucy it registered big with me how much fun and connection she and Jim had that day. Then I confessed my feelings of jealousy and insecurity about her paying him so much attention and maybe falling for him.

Lucy was completely surprised by my negative feelings and firmly reassured me that, yes, he was a likeable and fun person to be around but I was "the man" and she loved me. She emphasized, "You're the guy I married aren't you?"

The monster evaporated and was replaced by a sense of relief and a feeling of confidence that I was the one.

Later I realized this situation was a good example of my having acted on Perls' meaning of responsibility—"the ability to respond." When I responded to my catastrophic fantasies by sharing my negative emotions with Lucy, I took responsibility for my fears and got her real feelings. The only way I know to undo a false belief or a "mind read" is to check it out with the person onto whom you've projected your imaged truth.

A popular Christian book, *The Shack* (Windblown Media, 2007) uses Perls' concept in a spiritual way: The Holy Spirit in the guise of an Asian woman, Sarayu, says to the protagonist:

> *Then let's use your two words: responsibility and expectation. Before your words became nouns, they were first my words, nouns with movement and experience buried inside of them; the ability to respond and expectancy. My*

words are alive and dynamic—full of life and possibility; yours are dead, full of law and fear and judgment. That is why you won't find the word responsibility in the Scriptures. . . . I give you an ability to respond and your response is to be free to love and serve in every situation, and therefore each moment is different and unique and wonderful. Because I am your ability to respond, I have to be present in you. If I simply gave you a responsibility, I would not have to be with you at all. It would now be a task to perform, an obligation to be met, something to fail.

Changing the meaning of an event by reframing it

John Hoover

Recently I've been considering the term "reframe" and how frequently we use it in counseling.

Since "re-" means "again," then "reframe" means "to frame again." Just as pictures have frames around them, so do our ideas and thoughts. A frame surrounds a picture like a frame of reference surrounds our ideas. Therefore, it is the context around some idea that puts the idea into a perspective. Just as a well-selected picture frame enhances features in the picture, one's frame around an idea enhances the features in an idea that you want emphasized. Even the tone of our language or the expression on our face helps frame the ideas that we are presenting.

Our minds are meaning-making machines. Because of the way our minds work, we automatically, instantly have perspectives about many things that are taking place in our lives.

Any event has the potential of being seen in a variety of ways. Take for example the time I got a message at my office that a scheduled workshop that I was to lead the next day was cancelled due to a lack of enrollment. My frame of reference went from "Whew! I'm relieved, I wasn't really prepared," to "Oh, no, nobody wants to be in my workshop. I'm not good enough."

My clients come to me with personal stories of their lives. They give accounts of how they were treated or mistreated and, as they do so, they often reveal emotional stuck points that have not been successfully processed or talked out enough to have relief. Upon hearing the stories and seeing the emotions in my clients, I might focus on that emotion empathically so as to encourage that person to express that feeling more deeply. On the other hand, I might instead respond to this client with a question such as "What did that mean to you?"

At the cognitive level we are asking for the client to report the perspective or point of view they held about what was going on at the time. In so doing, the purpose is to explore a different frame of reference or perspective (reframing) that can result in a change of meaning of that event and thereby can bring about a change in the emotional reaction as well.

Being able to look back or reflect on a situation in one's life allows for an individual to both respect the response or reaction that they

45

had while being able to look at it from a variety of different useful perspectives. It is a way of discerning how one's thoughts or actions in that moment were based on the meaning that their mind instantly provided

It might be helpful here to distinguish between what I call a "reaction" and what I call a "response." By "response" I mean that there is a moment of rational, cognitive awareness in which one's mind interprets the present event based entirely on what is going on in the moment and which then leads to action appropriate for the circumstances.

A "reaction" occurs when one's mind summons up a previous package of thought and feeling that had applied to an earlier event similar to the present, and leads to reacting (acting again) in ways not appropriate for the present circumstances.

I'd like to relate a reframing experience with a client who as a 10-year-old witnessed her father brutally attacking her mother on more than one occasion. Her mother decided to leave her husband. Taking her two children with her and without telling her husband, she made arrangements with a friend in a distant state to temporarily shelter her.

The man who lived next door had been aware of the abuse and drove the mother and children several states away to the friend's house. However, the mother's friend, based on her Catholic beliefs, decided that the right thing to do was to alert the husband to his wife's plan. The husband immediately caught a flight and got there before his wife arrived.

My client described the scene. When mother and children arrived by car they were confronted by the screaming, rage-aholic husband, (my client's father), threatening to kill the neighbor who had driven them to this location. When my client witnessed this moment, she froze in abject terror, feeling helpless, powerless, and overwhelmed. She thought everyone was going to be killed.

In our session my client reported that she felt guilt and shame because she froze. "I hated that I didn't do anything; I just stayed frozen. And that's how I handle anger whenever I am confronted with it . . . ever since that happened."

After we did some work to reframe this experience, I asked her to look again at herself as the 10-year-old child and to notice exactly what she did in that situation from a more objective perspective. My client noticed that what she did was probably the wisest thing possible to do for her own safety as well as the safety of others.

Even though it was an unconscious act to freeze, my client couldn't think of a conscious choice that a 10-year-old might have made that would have been any wiser. Suddenly her eyes flew wide open and almost with delight she blurted out, "I did the right thing! That wasn't the wrong thing after all. I wasn't guilty of anything. I didn't need to feel shame."

As this refreshing new perspective flashed across her face she realized that she was not really helpless and powerless in a sense, but she in fact did "something" that turned out to be not just appropriate, but wise. She also saw that the length of time of being "frozen" was but a moment . . . not in perpetuity, and she did "handle" this intense trauma sufficiently.

In this example of my client's trauma, her reactive beliefs of being powerless to do anything in the face of anger triggered that reactive pattern which occurred whenever she faced anger from then on. Therefore it was helpful for her to experience seeing that same exact situation from a different perspective, to reframe it. Armed with this positive reframe, she then became free from her self-defeating and long-held beliefs and started on a journey of experiencing more of her own power and confidence in difficult and stressful situations.

Huff and puff, piss and moan

John Hoover & Eli Mitchell

Eli: Resistance is one of those ever-present conditions that causes so much psychological misery, and I see some form of it almost everyday in my life. Today for instance, I intended to get up and do a two-mile jog, but the weather was overcast and gloomy. I was thinking "I don't want to go out there; I'll jog tomorrow." Now that's just plain resistance. The minute I entertain the thought of gloomy weather, I instantly feel heavy and sluggish. I know my mind is causing that lethargic feeling, so I need to use my mind to create a different set of feelings. Know what I mean, John?

John: Oh, yes, that's so classic. It sometimes seems that the mind doesn't want any bodily effort to be expended. It's always looking for excuses to sit back, go on automatic, and cruise along without discomfort. That's why we often have to create disciplines to keep us focused on our tasks and objectives that require sustained effort.

Eli: Because otherwise our mind jumps in and thinks: "That's too much work!"

John: That reminds me of a time when my wife, Sharon, David Hoffman, and I were hiking in the Superstition Mountains near Phoenix, Arizona. After walking for about a mile-and-a-half on a beautiful desert trail named Hackberry Springs Trail, we came to a high ridge from which the trail ahead could be seen winding down in a big arch into the vast sea of arid desert. David said to Sharon, "See that little patch of green way down there? That's Hackberry Springs." Sharon asked, "Are we going down there?" David answered, "Well, the thing is if we walk all the way down there, we'll have to walk all the way back up here." Sharon said, "Yeah, so?" David answered, "Well, that's a lot of huffing and puffing and pissing and moaning." Sharon tilted her head in David's direction, shrugged her shoulders, and with smiling eyes said, "The huffing and puffing's OK."

David, who is also a psychologist and workshop trainer, often tells this story about Sharon's suggestion to him on the Hackberry Springs Trail. He tells people how it changed his thinking. David says that until that moment he had never walked up hills without this incessant, complaining monologue. In fact, he admitted that it wasn't just about walking up hills that elicited deep resistance. A lot of activities that required effort fell into that same category. It was as if effort and resistance always go together; you know, huffing and puffing equals pissing and moaning. For David it was literally a paradigm shift. He was now able to see huffing and puffing as an acceptable physical activity that didn't need mental resistance added to it. He saw the pissing and moaning as simply an added-on, unnecessary state of mind. Our mind, of course, is the place of origin where resistance is created. The body creates huffing and puffing, but the mind creates pissing and moaning—in a word, misery!

Eli: I'm remembering a therapy one-liner: "Whatever we resist persists." If you're feeling annoyed, angry, miserable, and you resist those feelings, you will keep feeling those feelings. You just keep it all inside and continue to feel miserable and annoyed. If what you're feeling is scared and you try not to feel scared, that is, you resist the feelings of being scared, you will continue to feel scared. If you're sad and you don't allow yourself to weep, you'll be sad for a long time. Whatever we resist persists.

John: I think that's one we just keep learning over and over again.

Eli: An example just popped into my mind, and I feel some chagrin about it.

John: Good. So, would you be willing to tell me about it?

Eli: Nice, Hoover, you whipped right into the therapist role didn't you!

John: Yeah, yeah, I thought you'd appreciate that.

Eli: OK, I will tell on myself with this little vignette. After a visit with my wife's parents in Clarkston, Michigan, Lucy and I drove home to Knoxville. We had a conflict before we left that morning wherein Lucy had expressed her side of our disagreement and had emotionally moved on. For me, the issue remained unresolved, and I decided to clam up. Throughout the day's drive, Lucy made several positive attempts to get me out of my clam shell, to no avail. When we stopped for lunch Lucy invited me to join her in the restaurant, but I declined and stayed in the car with clenched teeth, a straight-ahead stare, and arms tightly folded across my chest.

By the time we got home from Michigan, some thirteen hours later, I was still in the clutches of anger, completely worn out, and uncertain of what our disagreement was actually about! I had proven what I already knew intellectually—what you resist (in this case—resentment) persists, for sure.

John: So the other side of the coin of "what we resist persists" is what happens when we don't resist. If you are feeling sad, and you sit down and have a good cry, your experience of sadness will diminish and disappear. That sad emotional energy will change. It's likely to be replaced with a sense of relief and calm. It's the same with any emotion, negative or positive.

If you express the emotion, the emotion moves on and out. So the other side of the coin of "whatever we resist persists" is "whatever we experience disappears!" That means that when we fully experience the emotion it is emptied. The energy of that emotion is gone. To fully experience an emotion is to allow one's body to be open to the organismic pattern that the body naturally takes, including the sounds that go with it.

Eli: Absolutely. I remember one time I happened to be home one mid-afternoon when my then eight-year-old daughter, Tina, got off the school bus, ran into the house, threw down her book-bag, and burst into tears. I put her onto my lap, hugged her, and asked, "What happened?" Tearfully she wailed, "I dropped my tray at lunch." "Oh that's too bad," I said. Pause. "Anything else?" Still sobbing Tina replied, "I forgot to study for a test and I flunked it." A few minutes more of crying. Then she perked up, wiped away her tears and said, "Let's go outside and play."

John: Yep, just like that, she expressed her emotional energy which returned her to a place of peace and calm.

Emotions: E-motions

Eli Mitchell & John Hoover

John: Let's start our speaking about human emotion—or the "motion" of emotions—with your metaphor: Anxiety is Like Life in a Bomb Shelter.

Eli: A former client's story inspired this metaphor. She spoke of her teen years as being full of anxiety because she had to contend with an alcoholic father:

> *It was like an air raid siren would go off every weekday evening around 6:00 o'clock when my father was expected home from work. Some evenings it was a false alarm because Dad would be sober and loving. However, many nights the bombs dropped . . . my father would be drunk, mean, and abusive to Mom and me.*

To our detriment, we can react to life as if we are living in a bomb shelter. Often in our thoughts we might hear the siren sounding and, whether a false alarm or not, we "get ready" (aroused to fight or flee) for the bombs—our heart pounds, our palms sweat, our breathing becomes shallow, et cetera.

John: And all other mammals respond quite differently. The grizzly apparently does not get uptight about possibly meeting a person on the trail. If they do have an encounter, you can bet the bear will attack. A deer probably doesn't fret about a hunter being in a tree stand near its salt lick; however, if the deer gets a whiff of one, she takes off running.

Since we Homo sapiens can anticipate the future, we have great potential to sabotage ourselves. We create our anxieties by thinking about, and thereby gearing way up for, a challenge (even a positive one) that is not present yet, or even for one that never materializes.

Eli: As you know, John, Fritz Perls, the developer of Gestalt therapy, framed our typical interpersonal anxieties as stage fright. When we are in a new social situation or called on to "perform" in some way, we might think like Shakespearean actors of old, "Will I get applause, or will I get rotten eggs?" Hereby, we create our experience of anxiety.

John: As a consultant to TVA, I met with about 12 mid-level managers to help them develop more self-awareness and better communication skills. As usual (like psychologists tend to do), we set up the chairs so that all of us were seated in a circle. At the initial meeting, after introducing myself, I asked the managers to go around the circle and say their name and specific job description. As they proceeded, I asked them to notice any build-up of tension in their body before it was their time to share. I explained it was normal to experience some anxiety even if the challenge is minimal.

About halfway around the circle, one manager said he didn't feel any tension or anxiety at all. As a matter of fact, he never felt uptight even as he spoke in front of large audiences, which he often did. On the other hand, he admitted that on occasion at the podium he would suddenly pass out. Didn't know why!

At that time, I acknowledged this manager's truth. After the meeting I met with him and coached him on how to be more bodily aware and how to better handle his anxiety before it "knocked him out."

Eli: Good going. Lesson learned: if we are not aware of our physical experience (especially anxiety) and consequently we don't know how to manage it, it can rule us.

John: Speaking of anxiety, the most common phobia in psychological literature is the fear of public speaking. One possible way to defuse public speaking anxiety is to "own" your uptightness with the audience. For example, you might say "I'm excited and a bit nervous talking to you today, and . . ." or, "I want to let you know I'm both eager and anxious about speaking to you this morning, so please bear with me."

Eli: It is interesting, isn't it, John, the same physiological response that occurs with our excitement such as rapid heart rate and rapid breathing, occurs with our anxiety. We label which emotion we are feeling based on our present circumstances. Rage is the frozen emotion.

Rage is possibly the most dangerous human emotion. When it is unhindered in its expression it becomes pressed-out rage—outrage. The feeling of total helplessness is a feeding frenzy for the buildup of rage. When that rage is expressed, it comes out in senseless violence.

> ### Fire And Ice
>
> *Some say the world will end in fire,*
> *Some say in ice.*
> *From what I've tasted of desire*
> *I hold with those who favor fire.*
> *But if it had to perish twice,*
> *I think I know enough of hate*
> *To say that for destruction ice*
> *Is also great*
> *And would suffice.*
>
> –Robert Frost (1923)

John: Oh, yeah, the fear or experience of being helpless shifts into violence and aggression. I'm reminded of the tragedy you've spoken of in which a man murdered three people at the Tennessee Valley Unitarian Universalist Church in Knoxville a few years ago.

Also, I'm remembering in 1966 a young man, armed with a high-powered rifle, climbed the tower on the University of Texas campus and randomly shot and killed people below in cold blood. Evidently he felt like a nobody and therefore took out his rage on innocent victims.

Eli: The concept of "in cold blood" reminds me of how the medieval Italian poet Dante described the last circle of hell. In his *Divine Comedy: Inferno* in this final round of Hades, sinners are completely encased in ice and contorted into all sorts of positions. For Dante they suffer thusly in this frozen fate because on earth they were guilty of treachery, the ultimate sin of malice.

John: So people who are hateful and are frozen with rage can be seen as experiencing hell on earth!

Turning fear into anger

Eli: On a more positive note, John, tell about turning your fear into anger; you know, the story about your misadventure with a pack of dogs.

John: Oh yeah, I sure do remember that one. Going home on leave in the Marine Corps I was trying to hitch-hike a ride sometime after midnight carrying my duffle bag. As I was walking on the road through the outskirts of Winston-Salem, several dogs started barking. One by one a pack of dogs began forming. They were coming from distant unlit houses and began to slowly approach me. I was becoming quite scared and tried to act friendly, you know, "nice doggie, nice doggie." They became more aggressive by growling, barking, snarling, and pressing closer, teeth bared. "Stay!" "Sit!" "C'mere, boy." They kept on growling and moving in.

I was now terrified. They were like a gang egging each other on for an attack. Suddenly the pure fright in me flipped into an explosion of aggressive adrenalin. I let go my duffle bag and lunged at them. In a flash in my mind I saw grabbing the closest snarling dog and smashing him to the pavement and using his dead body to kill every other dog in the pack. When they turned and ran yelping in all directions, I actually wanted to go after them. It was crazy! It's what we mean when we refer to someone who has flipped out! I was nuts!

Once I finally calmed down, I picked up my duffle bag and hoofed it a mile or so before someone finally picked me up.

Eli: Wow, that's quite a story. It illustrates that even though we can't decide to change instantly how we feel, sometimes our instincts will do that for us, particularly if we are in a fight or flight survival mode. In most circumstances however, we can decide to change our behavior, and when we do, our feelings typically follow the change. In your misadventure your feelings and behavior flipped from flight to fight; that is clearly one of those deeply imbedded survival strategies that is triggered by intense fear. At the point of terror your instinct went from fear to fierce!

Getting "unstuck" from guilt

John Hoover

When I was an intern at the University of Texas, Psychological Services Center, we all had to take a bunch of psychological assessments as part of the internship. This process was intended, in part, to familiarize us with many of the most popular psych tests, and to hear a professional interpretation given individually by the director of the testing service.

When I scored in the 99th percentile on a scale that measures guilt, the director and I both agreed that perhaps I might want to deal with that in therapy pretty quickly! Since I spent quite some time on that topic in therapy, I can readily relate to clients who struggle with issues of guilt.

One such client was Bill, who had come to me about his relationship with Betty, a woman that he was considering marrying. Bill was conflicted. His struggle had to do with guilt that he was still carrying from his previous marriage. Bill had had an affair that precipitated the divorce of that first marriage, and the moldy, old guilt was interfering with his ability to make a decision about marrying Betty.

When I asked Bill how long ago it was since he'd had his affair, he said seven years, and that he has felt guilt every day since. I asked him if he would like to stop feeling guilty, and he said yes. So I suggested to him that he could trade in guilt for responsibility. You see, rather than owning his indiscretion, rather than taking full responsibility for what he had done and for the consequences of the affair, he had instead continued to condemn, blame, and punish himself, and thereby remain irresponsible. It's sort of like he'd split himself into the blamer and into the blamed, which kept him from incorporating his irresponsible act into his life. The blamer voice inside him would beat him up and scare him with accusations like:

> *If I tell Betty she'll run.*
>
> *I was such an idiot.*
>
> *I don't have any self-control.*
>
> *I had an affair.*
>
> *I knew better.*
>
> *I ruined everything.*

I'm bad; no one would want me now.

My wife left me because of it, so no one would want to marry me now.

I can't trust myself that I wouldn't do it again.

It's hopeless.

Betty deserves better.

I'm a loser.

Bill believed that he couldn't tell Betty because she was still angry that her first husband had cheated on her, thus precipitating their divorce.

In order to move forward with his life, it was essential that Bill tell himself the truth about his affair and release himself from his unrelenting self-condemnation.

So I wrote all of those accusations up on my white board. Then we went over each statement verifying each one to be true, false, or don't know, as taught in the More to Life Program. As I suspected, his internal blamer had not uttered a single truth except "I had an affair." All the rest of the statements were judgments, opinions, or predictions, none of which had any verifiable existence in reality.

I then asked Bill to just tell me the truth about the affair. I supported him to fully own all of his actions, without toxic shame, claiming full responsibility for what beliefs and justifications he had created that allowed him to engage in an affair. When he began to take ownership of his actions, he shifted from "I am guilty of having an affair," to "I am responsible for having an affair." The tone of his voice, his facial expression, and his posture noticeably shifted from that of a bad little boy, to that of a man with genuine, adult regret.

I then asked him what he chose to do with this newly-discovered truth. He immediately answered, first, tell Betty and second, declare his intention to never have that occur again. He looked and sounded relieved. The postscript to this story is that he did tell Betty, and she did understand. Some months later they married.

Posttraumatic stress disorder

Eli Mitchell & John Hoover

Eli: John, Posttraumatic Stress Disorder (PTSD) is a complicated syndrome and deserves a lot of attention.

John: Considering that about 25 percent of people who survive significant traumatic events develop PTSD, it's definitely a topic of considerable importance.

Eli: And add to that fact—the majority of people on this planet will indeed experience an extremely traumatic event at least once in their lifetime.

John: You're recognized as one of the most skilled professionals in trauma work in this region, Eli. Your work with combat veterans, 9/11 survivors, Katrina evacuees, and the American Red Cross marks you as an expert in the disaster recovery field. Say some things about who is likely to develop PTSD. And what distinguishes something as a psychological trauma versus a disturbing event with or without physical injury?

Eli: The type of events that give rise to PTSD can be defined in two broad categories:

- those involving person-to-person violence; and
- those involving potentially life-threatening accidents and disasters, either man made or naturally occurring, that happen in the absence of a conscious attempt of one person to harm others.

The defining characteristics of these events are their ability to provoke an intense psychological response. It is the threat of injury or death and the attendant feelings of fear, helplessness, or horror that initiate the biological responses leading to PTSD.

John: Yes, that certainly fits with my experience of helping clients dealing with their traumas. Sometimes PTSD occurs when an individual witnesses or just learns about another's trauma, especially if the victim is a loved one.

Eli: Since we both work a lot in what I call the psytrauma recovery field, let's relate a few episodes that might shed some light on exactly what PTSD is like and how we work with those in therapy to make it less intense.

I wrote the following poem based on a client's actual combat experience in the 1991 Persian Gulf War and his prolonged flashback drama thirteen years later.

WAR WOUNDS

The Gulf War tendered no wounds to flesh or bone.
The worst of it was the midnight tank battle.
Barrage. Strobe lights. Concussions.
Radios quit. Bayonet in hand,
Dan leaps out, desperate to shout
"Keep moving, take no prisoners."
An Iraqi rises from the sand.
Dan impales his gut, rides him down.
Gun flashes reveal whiskered, sunken cheeks.
His father's face.

Thirteen years pass.
Home in the mountains,
Dan is high in a hemlock
Cutting dead limbs.
Chainsaw dust flies in his eyes,
Desert sand.
Oily gas smells of diesel fuel,
Billowing wells.
The crack of a branch,
Rifle fire.
Dan shouts to helmeted ghosts,
"Take cover," slings his saw
And plunges. . . .

The Medivac chopper glides

Dan and his father over foothills

While his fear hovers:

The Iraqis will shoot us down.

Dad's plaintive whisper,

"Son, its two thousand and four

You're home from the war."

Dan mutters, "I'm sorry, I'm sorry."

John: I notice your excellent poem makes clear two important dynamics that occur in the unconscious mind after a traumatic event. First, the post-traumatized mind cannot tell the difference between "similar" and "same." For this veteran small chips from his chainsaw is Persian Gulf desert sand. And the saw's gas and oil mixture smells to him exactly like both Army tank exhaust and burning Iraqi oil wells.

Second, the traumatized unconscious doesn't differentiate between "past" and "present." The stimuli of "sand" and "diesel smell' caused Dan to re-experience the tank battle that took place in 1991.

Eli: That's right, John. In addition, I mentioned earlier that his flashback was prolonged; that's because the medical helicopter evacuation (University of Tennessee Medical Center's Lifestar helicopter) unfortunately reminded him of watching some of his wounded comrades being medivaced during the war.

John: As you know, PTSD is considered to be the "mother" of the anxiety disorders since this diagnosis includes numerous symptoms from every category of anxiety disorder. For example, PTSD has elements of panic, phobic, and dysthymic disorders.

Let's discuss more illustrations of the three main dynamics of PTSD: re-experiencing, hyperarousal, and avoidance. For starters, your poem is an outstanding example of showing the intensity of a flashback, which is often an element in re-experiencing.

Eli: And flashbacks can last for only a few seconds or for hours and hours. Plus as you know, flashbacks can be re-experienced with all five of our senses.

Moving on to the dynamic of hyperarousal, an Army Reserve combat veteran related an unsettling experience he had in a local cafeteria some months after returning from active duty in Iraq. As he was sitting alone at a table, the waitress accidently dropped her pile of trays behind him. He was under the table in about two seconds.

John: The exaggerated startle response can flat "own" you! Present reality is replaced with past reality—bypassing all logic and common sense. Also, one episode like that and the veteran might become avoidant and never enter that cafeteria or any restaurant, for that matter, again.

Eli: So true. Here's a story about overcoming avoidance. To help my client, Angela, recover from a bus wreck trauma—in addition to using Eye Movement Desensitization and Reprocessing (EMDR) as well as some Neuro-Lingustic Programming (NLP) techniques—I asked Angela to set up a graduated exposure desensitization exercise.

John: That would be where Angela would be progressively exposed to the situation she had become phobic of until she could finally tolerate it, right?

Eli: Right. So in her junior year in high school Angela was among a group of students riding in a bus, driven by a woman, that turned into the path of a tractor-trailer rig. Her favorite female teacher and one student were killed. After this horrendous crash, an injured Angela heroically tried to perform CPR on her dying teacher—to no avail.

Angela came to see me for psychotherapy six months after the wreck because, as you might imagine, she still was dealing with several serious PTSD symptoms including frequent nightmares, insomnia, and severe depression, as well as high anxiety and flashbacks, especially when she rode in or drove a car.

After we were able to reduce the intensity of those symptoms, it became foreground for Angela to deal with her strong avoidance for riding in buses—not only school buses but any bus, such as a city or tour bus. She had planned a trip to France that summer and was afraid she would be too fearful to ride on the tour bus—the main mode of transportation for her European adventure.

Angela was a valued member of her school's swim team but could not make herself ride on the team bus. Therefore she drove herself, following the bus, to any swim-team meets off-campus. This, of course, was a source of embarrassment for Angela but a necessity in her current state.

John: So trauma recovery methods like EMDR and NLP were helpful but as far as you could tell they didn't touch the "avoidance of bus rides" issue.

Eli: Correct. So Angela and I designed and enacted a graduated desensitization plan. It was easy for Angela to get school personnel "on board," so to speak.

First, Angela, accompanied by a female teacher, got on a parked school bus, sat sharing a candy bar and talking for five or so minutes, then exited the bus. The next week Angela and her teacher got on the bus together, and a male bus driver drove them around for about 10 minutes. Finally, the following week, those three rode the bus together for some 15 minutes. Angela reported that her anxiety was "somewhat further diminished" after each bus exercise. She didn't ride a bus again until she went to France with some of her graduate class and a female teacher, who happened to be a close friend of Angela's deceased teacher.

John: How did that subsequent European bus tour go?

Eli: Angela did OK. In spite of some moderate anxiety, she was able to travel on all of the bus tours. It helped that her teacher/chaperone was understanding of her phobic responses and accommodated any proposals that made Angela more comfortable. For example, her teacher made sure Angela, per her request, always rode on the right (non-collision) side of the bus and not in the same seat as in the wreck.

John: Your psychotherapy with Angela ended in January, 1999. Have you heard from her since then?

Eli: Glad you asked. We had a long phone conversation in May 2010; she's doing extremely well. Angela has earned a PharmD degree and was to complete her Residency training by the end of that June. She said, "Career opportunities abound."

John: Any residual PTSD from her trauma over twelve years ago?

Eli: Nothing that really gets in her way. When confronted with situations that might require her to perform CPR, she has experienced a few seconds of a visual flashback. Otherwise, she's a free bird!

PTSD: Multiple traumatic experiences versus a single trauma

Eli: John, I've found that psychotherapy with PTSD clients who have suffered a series of traumas—I call this a "trauma drama"—is much more problematical than working with a single event like Angela's bus wreck. The victims of repeated child abuse fall into this category of suffering from tenacious symptoms. Also, the PTSD symptoms of combat veterans I've seen from World War II and the Vietnam, Gulf, or Iraqi wars have been especially intransigent.

John: I'm aware that the war veterans you are talking about are traumatized in combat over and over to different degrees over a period of months and sometimes years.

Eli: Oh, yes. Therefore, in many cases the best I could do was to assist the vet in reducing the symptomatic impact of their worst traumatic episodes. A case in point is a Vietnam vet and our work with his reoccurring nightmare.

Tony sought me out to get some relief from his serious PTSD symptoms. He was a highly-decorated combat soldier, including being awarded a Purple Heart, who was experiencing classical PTSD symptoms forty years after his military service.

When we first began working together, almost every night Tony was haunted by intense, reoccurring nightmares related to the many traumas he suffered through in Nam such as firefights, being wounded, buddies killed, et cetera. He typically awoke in a cold-sweat, panic mode.

His worse reoccurring nightmare basically unfolded as follows.

> *Two Military Policemen come into my house and tell me I have to go back to Vietnam. I protest that I already spent a year in combat in Nam and I've been discharged from the Army for years. They refused to listen and insist I go with them. Suddenly I am back to a familiar base in Vietnam. . . .*

The rest of this nightmare varies, but the thread is the same: dead VC bodies, firefights, out of ammo, useless weapons, and intense fear.

John: What was your strategy to lessen the impact of those war dream scenarios?

Eli: Since dreams, especially nightmares, are mostly or totally from the unconscious, Tony and I set out to defuse this specific reoccurring nightmare by making its various images as conscious as possible.

For months-on-end some part of our therapy sessions was spent bringing this disturbing dream more into consciousness through different processes such as EMDR, retelling the dream repeatedly, running the scenes forward and backward (NLP submodality work), and so on.

After sixteen-or-so months of consistently working on this dream, it changed significantly for the better. The first scene featuring the MP visit and abduction dropped out completely. The experience of intense fear and the disturbing scenes of war occurring in-country occurred far less often.

62

John: Sounds like you are doing what you can to help remediate some very old, deeply-rooted wounds. As you said, Eli, it is a complicated syndrome.

Eli: I am still working with Tony, and his nightmares are less frequent. Unfortunately his dreams remain plagued with the dynamic of running out of ammunition and gun malfunction. We figure these two issues are more resistant to change because the most traumatic event Tony experienced was when he was involved in a four-hour night battle wherein he was totally out of ammunition for a few minutes—long enough to think he was surely going to die.

John: There are so many things running through my mind about this story. Forty years later the trauma "node" in Tony's brain still contains the negative emotional impact of that event. It was too much, too big for his mind to digest at the time. What a complex organ is our brain. What a complex processor is our mind. PTSD seems to be our vital mental survival mechanisms gone awry.

Philosophically, I wonder when are we, as a species, going to learn to settle differences between each other in ways that respect the sanctity of life! Nobody, no country, no faction of people can emerge from war without losing something precious about their nobility. When we are reduced to killing one another we have stopped seeing the truth of our oneness as beings.

As an evolving species we must embrace our higher consciousness that knows about the mutual and reciprocal contributions we can make to benefit the "highest good" for the whole of humanity. We have to learn to see that if we are for our own benefit without simultaneously being for others, we have created "separation" between us and them. At some point in our evolution "us and them" has to stop. That species' time on the planet is term-limited! We can either become more evolved beings or be like the Neanderthals who preceded us Homo sapiens. It is literally a choice that our survival depends on.

PATHS TO WHOLENESS

Working with our dreams

Eli Mitchell

It was during my very first Gestalt experience that I realized how powerful dreamwork could be in understanding one's dreams. I attended a group psychotherapy conference in 1970 in San Francisco to honor Fritz Perls, who died earlier that year. In a small-group experiential demonstration lead by Dr. Eric Marcus, a first generation Gestalt therapist who had trained with Perls, I volunteered to work on a reoccurring nightmare . . . an unsettling dream I experienced every few months since my 1966 discharge from active duty as a Navy officer. (I had served three years on board the *USS Valcour* [AGF1], a ship homeported in the Persian Gulf.)

The main disturbing image in the dream had me in command of the ship (I was the officer of the deck.) and another ship sliced into my ship's side and split us in two. Earlier, I was giving this nightmare a Freudian analytic spin—thinking it had to do with castration anxiety. After hearing my dream, Dr. Marcus instructed me to make a round (meaning to go around the group speaking to each person in the group individually) and complete the sentence stem, "I am responsible for . . ." So I proceeded to say, "I am responsible for speaking to you." Next person, "I am responsible for my life." And so on until soon I experienced an "Aha!" This dream was about responsibility anxiety, not castration anxiety.

In reality, being the officer of the deck while the *Valcour* was underway always created a state of anxiety in me since the lives of some two hundred men were at stake as well as my reputation for competence as the guy-in-charge. What came out of that brief Gestalt work was that once I owned that I was responsible for both my actions and my anxiety, I was grounded (though not in the sense that a ship is grounded!). Since I integrated the message of the dream's theme, I never had that nightmare again.

Besides the "here and now" experience of Gestalt therapy, the above dreamwork also demonstrates how a Gestaltist goes for: "Where is the conflict energy? What is the theme? And, how can an insight come about?"

Gestalt therapists avoid "analysis paralysis" at all cost; they lead clients toward "striking a match" rather than "shining a flashlight."

I heard about a psychiatrist who would elicit a patient's dream and then tell them he would let them know what their dream meant in the next session . . . a big "No-No" in my judgment! Clients know much more about their dreams than we ever will. Our job is to facilitate awareness as best we can. I might offer my hunch to a client about their dream but never an interpretation.

Since dream studies show that typically we have four to five dreams per eight hours of sleep, our challenge is to recall the more salient ones in order to gain more self-awareness, empowerment, direction, and even spiritual insight.

The *Talmud* says, "A dream that is not understood is like a letter left unopened." For me, that means a dream may be as salient as a letter from a long lost friend, or as unremarkable as an overdue utility bill.

To get the theme/meaning of a dream, we don't have to remember every detail. On the other hand, even a dream segment might be a vital scrap of a map to a treasure one has been seeking.

To be more aware of our consciousness, an instructive analogy is how our mind can be compared to a rubber ball floating on water. Much of this ball is always underwater (our unconsciousness), however, the ball can be spun so that some of what had been unconscious becomes conscious.

The more dramatic, outrageous, and irrational (even bizarre) that dreams—especially nightmares—are, the more likely they are purely from our unconscious. And becoming more conscious of this psychic material that was "underwater" can be life-changing.

Unlike Freud's contention that the truths we learn from dreams are "disguised" and therefore difficult to grasp, dreams, in a symbolic or metaphorical way, typically exaggerate the issues they present to the dreamer. A quick example: Say I dream that my best friend is literally and graphically stabbing me in the back, and I awaken greatly distressed. This could be a metaphor indicating that he might be doing something hurtful to me behind my back. Another possibility is that I am both villain and victim and am somehow being self-destructive.

Some dreams can be so obvious that it's easy to miss their message. When working on a dream with a client, I ask them to relate it to me, start to finish, in as much detail as possible. As they tell their dream, I ask them to notice associations that "bubble up" into consciousness, no matter how seemingly unrelated.

Now, dreams tend to be elusive to grasp, so to record them when they're fresh is essential. On occasion, I have awakened early in the morning, jotted down a dream and then gone back to sleep. The next day I have been pleasantly surprised to discover a written-out dream that had evaporated from my memory.

Here are three tips on dream-catching:

1. Keep a pen and paper or a voice recorder by your bed to immediately capture a dream.

2. Have the word DREAM written out in bright letters and in sight, right before bedtime.

3. Before sleep, make a request (not a demand) to self, or to your Higher Power, that you have a meaningful dream and that you remember it first thing in the morning.

Once I ask clients to record their dreams, most comply. Even the clients that say they seldom or never recall a dream often will produce one if encouraged.

I consider Dr. Ann Faraday's book, *The Dream Game*, a classic in the field because it makes dreamwork accessible to the layperson as well as to the professional. An experimental psychologist, Faraday grounds her material in Jung's extensive formulations and Perls' Gestalt approach to dream insights.

To briefly summarize, Faraday contends dreams are directly related to the events and thoughts of the previous day or two. She developed a three-stage method to assist dreamers in interpreting their idiosyncratic dream world.

1. Literal—Example: The night before I was to give a lecture, I dreamed I was in front of my audience, shirtless. I was literally unprepared, got the dream's message, and that morning boned up on what I planned to say.

2. How we are feeling about people or external situations—usually analogies or metaphors. Example: my "stabbing me in the back" dream above.

3. Looking completely inward at our psyche—Its conflicts, its beauty, its beasts, even its soul. Example: my possession/shadow/compensation dream.

It's fascinating how Jung postulated that archetypes, that is, original models or patterns from which all things of the same kind are based, are universally present in individual psyches . . . and that they are "collectively inherited," therefore, the term "the collective unconscious."

An apt metaphor is that the collective (or universal) unconscious is like a vast underground stream that sources all individual wells (every human psyche).

Spiritual dreams

To begin my speaking about spiritual dreams, I'll quote Scripture, Job 33: 14-16.

For God does speak—now one way,

now another—

though man may not perceive it.

In a dream, in a vision of the night,

when deep sleep falls on men

as they slumber in their beds,

he may speak in their ears

and terrify them with warnings. . .

From my Christian perspective, a spiritual dream occurs when The Holy Spirit appears to influence the dream material in a numinous way that transcends our ordinary reality, our ego, and even our consciousness. Themes that occur in spiritual dreams include those of transformation, redemption, healing, reconciliation, warnings, death, and rebirth. At times, it may be difficult to discern whether a dream has a spiritual meaning or not.

Kim, a female client in her thirties, told me that when she was a senior in high school, her boy friend committed suicide over the Christmas holidays. His loss affected her so deeply that she became depressed, could not go back to school, and instead stayed in her bedroom for days on end.

Then one night she dreamed:

I am in my car and suddenly my boy friend is sitting in the passenger seat right beside me. "I don't have much time here," he says as he points upward. "God might see me through that hole in the sky." Then he looks me in the eye, "Kim, I'm really OK. You need to go on with your life without me."

Kim said he then disappeared and she woke up. The very next morning Kim went back to school and began her life anew.

The following is another poignant dream with its positive consequences.

Nancy, a 70-year-old client, deals with high anxiety daily. She grew up in the Catholic faith and as an adult, she goes to a non-denominational church. One night she had this dream:

I am being carried by Jesus in his arms like one would carry a baby. I do not see His face but I know it is Him from pictures I've seen. He has strong, gangly arms and His waist is covered with a cloth. He looks to me like how He is shown in pictures. He's walking around with me in His arms and I feel so joyful, happy, safe, and secure. I've been happy many times in my life but never to this same degree. It's a peace and joy I've never felt before. Then I nestle my head on His chest. We never talk. He then stops walking, still holding me, and I say to Him, "Do it again," and He begins walking around again carrying me in his arms! I am ecstatic!

My thoughts when I wake up are sheer joy, peace, safety, contentment, and no fear or anxiety because Jesus is carrying me. What could be better than that? I am so grateful to Him and feel undeserving that He would do that for me, but very glad that He did. I think wow! I didn't even say "Please do it again." Who am I to tell my Lord what to do in a rude, demanding way? Oh, God forgive me and thanks.

* * *

I had an appointment with Dr. Mitchell to do Eye Movement Desensitization and Reprocessing (EMDR) regarding my medical anxieties the morning before my internist's appointment to check my blood pressure. I have hypertension and it's been getting worse. My medical doctor feels its anxiety related. I have been traumatized my whole life by fears of getting sick and/or having to go to the hospital.

Dr. Mitchell worked with me using EMDR and I visualized Jesus being with me. With therapeutic coaching, I relived the dream about Jesus carrying me, and I said over and over, "Jesus is with me." Then I imagined: He's holding my hand, He's walking with me to the doctors, He's sitting next to me in the doctor's office and in the examining room while my blood pressure is being taken.

When Nancy went to her appointment that afternoon, she did essentially what we had rehearsed a few hours earlier. Nancy, the nurse, and her doctor were astounded—her blood pressure was normal for the first time in ten years!

Empowerment generator

John Hoover

A few years back, I met with the entire staff of a car dealership at their facility. Roughly twenty-three people were present.

The outcome the owner of the dealership wanted was for his staff to be more inspired and to form clearer objectives for their departments. And word had it that Jeff, the parts department supervisor, was feeling notably uninspired!

In fact, he said, "How are you supposed to inspire people who come to work every day to do their ordinary job and it's just the same old work?"

At that point I had passed a sheet of paper out to everyone at the meeting asking them to write down what goal each of them had for the year. I asked Jeff to read aloud his goal for the parts department. He said "to do a better job of providing the mechanics and the customers with the correct part with minimal delay."

I said, "Fine."

Then he said "But that's not very inspiring and motivating is it?"

I said, "Well, Jeff, what would be the result if your department actually delivered the products to mechanics and customers more efficiently and effectively?"

He answered, "Well I'm sure they would like it."

I said, "OK, and what do you think would be the result of your mechanics and your customers liking it?"

He said, "Well Tom would like that for sure." And everybody laughed because Tom was the owner. And Tom laughed as well.

I responded, "And what would be the result of Tom liking it?"

He said, "When Tom's happy, everybody's happy." And again everybody laughed.

And I said, "What's that like for you when everybody's happy?"

Jeff responded, "Oh, I see, everybody feels better about working, just doing what they are doing."

And I said, "And what's the result of that . . . everybody feels better about working just doing what they are doing?"

Jeff said, "We get more work done, faster, we are friendlier, the day goes quicker, and we probably go home with a better attitude."

And I said, "What would it be like to actually come home with that kind of an attitude?"

Jeff said, "Well I know my kids and my wife would appreciate it." Again, everybody laughed. And of course I kept going.

So I said, "And what would be the result of that?"

Jeff said, "Well I guess it's obvious, everybody at home would have a better time together."

Then I asked, "What kind of a person would want everybody at home to have a better time together?"

Jeff said, "Someone like me . . . who puts his family first. And I try to do that here at work, too."

I asked, "What kind of person is it that not only wants family to have a better time but wants the people at work to have a better time as well?"

There was a pause as Jeff's eyes momentarily filled with tears, and he blinked a few times.

So I went on, "Imagine that caring energy happening here at work. What might it be like for customers who come in contact with any of the people in your department?"

Jeff smiled and said, "I get it, it's a ripple effect that impacts the lives of more people than we would even know about."

Then I had all of the participants divide into pairs and do an exercise with the empowerment generator that we'd just demonstrated.

The idea here is to translate an objection into an objective. That allows you to focus on a desired outcome so that when you ask what would be the result of getting that, it leads to a larger, more expanded perspective that includes their feelings about the desired outcome. Then the process naturally creates an outward expansion like concentric circles with the feelings getting larger as well. Any time that we are doing even a routine job, we can expand the perspective to empower our self to act from a higher level of nobility that exists within us.

In this manner, it's possible to add almost a spiritual dimension to a mundane task. It allows people to see that what they are doing is within a greater context than simply the task itself. We can see how the task can potentially affect the lives of others in positive ways that we may not have previously discerned.

Healing humor

Eli Mitchell

The movie *Patch Adams* (1998) is based on the heart-warming true story of an iconoclast who became a physician because he sincerely sought to help people heal using the power of laughter and humor. In fact, Patch dresses in a clown-like manner in his public appearances to this day.

It so happens Lucy and I have a loose connection to Patch. We are the proud god-parents of Lillie and Charlotte Huggins, the twenty-something daughters of my cousin, Andy. They frequently go on mission trips with Patch along with a group of clown volunteers from around the world. I recently spoke with Lillie and she said they have accompanied Patch's entourage to several countries including Haiti, Sri Lanka, Russia, and even Cuba.

Besides clowning around, however, these missions, sponsored by Patch's institute called Gesundheit!, are sophisticated humanitarian ventures that spread compassion, friendship, humor, and joy, that is—love. And love communicated through clowning and play transcends all language and cultural barriers. Lillie told me that being a clown in any country, especially a third world country, makes the "playing field" level. And clowning for adults, Lillie said, turns out to be even more impactful than playing with kids!

The numerous communities that Gesundeit! serves are all breeding grounds for suffering and loneliness: orphanages, nursing homes, refugee camps, hospitals, prisons, and even mental health facilities.

Lillie explained that the concept of Clown Care has been around since the mid-1980s. Clown Care programs have spread from the USA into Canada, Israel, and countries throughout Europe. These "clown doctors," in an atmosphere of fun and hope, not only help patients to heal—their humor is also beneficial to hospital staff and to the families of patients.

A classic book about how humor can be a healing force is *An Anatomy of an Illness* by Norman Cousins published in 1979.

Cousins was literally struck down by a supposedly untreatable, life-ruining disease. Working closely with his physician, Cousins actively shared in the responsibility for his day-to-day healing process. A holistic medicine approach involving large doses of Vitamin C and mega doses of laughter led to his rare and full recovery. One poignant early episode has Cousins, who is incapable of sitting up, flat on his back watching an old Marx Brothers movie being projected onto the ceiling!

Cousins opened a lot of people's eyes with his story of how he fully experienced the reality of his "terminal" medical condition. That he stopped resisting the actuality of his disease does not mean he gave up, threw in the towel . . . you win, I quit. He merely stopped resisting it, and that changed his relationship with the disease. In the middle of the dance, so to speak, Cousins changed how he was dancing with the disease. Right there on the dance floor facing the reality of dying, he shocked his dance partner with the dance of happiness.

> *Many of us think that happiness is not possible in the present moment. Most of us believe that there are a few more conditions that need to be met before we can be happy. The only moment for us to be alive in is the present moment. The past is already gone and the future is not yet here. Only in the present moment can we touch life and be deeply alive.*
>
> *–Thich Nhat Hanh, Be Free Where You Are* (Parallax Press, 2008)

According to Cousins, "I made the joyous discovery that ten minutes of genuine belly laughter had an anesthetic effect and would give me at least two hours of pain-free sleep." And he lived years longer than medical doctors predicted was possible.

A different kind of channeling

Eli Mitchell

In the 1980s, channeling was en vogue. Certain individuals went into an altered state and became "possessed" by an entity who was supposedly from a higher plane and who was wise, almost godlike.

Lately I have been playing around with a different kind of channeling—sort of like using your remote to change channels on your TV. Teaching clients to deliberately change channels is an effective way to assist them in reducing their negative thinking, especially if I am working with a person who wants to stop worrying excessively.

So what I do is suggest they change channels. If a client is obsessing about money, we might call that the K-MUD channel . . . M for money. I might encourage them to change to Channel K-ALM. On that channel, together we might develop a high definition (HD) video of a peaceful nature scene including Dolby surround sound.

Besides K-ALM, here are some other channel possibilities:

K-FUN: This could be a person's humor channel where they think of something funny and chuckle to themselves.

K-JOY: A channel that includes excitement about something or somebody. It certainly can be joyful to relate to a loved one, friend, or to one's higher power.

Then there's K-TASK, a channel that's about being in the here and now. As my wife Lucy's motto goes, "Focus, finish, feel good."

And then there's the channel I call K-PRAY—a channel having to do with harmony, meditation, prayer, and conscious contact with God.

Switching over to K-PRAY from channels considered sinful by Christians—such as jealousy, lust, and greed—should give one some relief from these worldly temptations.

Other channels from which to switch include resentment, depression, shame, and anxiety; also, any channel that has to do with our negative self-talk, that "crafty little sucker" (Brad Brown), or the "inner cruel critic" (Lewis Paul), which contributes to an inflated or deflated ego.

Most of us are familiar with the channel tuned to the ever popular "worst casing." I'm speaking of the awful scenarios that we can play out in our heads—what Perls labeled as "catastrophic thinking."

I've been very good at big-time catastrophic thinking. The following calamitous worrying occurred while I was visiting Germany on my way back to the USA from Persian Gulf military service. I had been recently accepted to the clinical psychology Graduate Program at the University of Tennessee and was very excited to have the possibility of earning a Ph.D.—a career dream since my high school days. The view from my tiny fourth-floor room in Munich was that of the English Gardens, a large grassy area full of rubble from buildings that had been bombed by the allies during World War II. Suddenly I had a feeling of dread at the dire thought there could be another war any time now and my choice career would be destroyed.

Another prevalent apprehension is the dynamic of "waiting for the other shoe to drop." When an adversity strikes, some of us expect something as bad or worse to occur soon after.

Amy, a client in her early thirties, described this self-defeating type of thought process as follows:

> *Since past good experiences always turned bad, I believed that any positive experience would always turn negative in the future. I expected things not to work out. I expected to be shocked and hurt by people. I expected to get scared and run away. I began to let those expectations ruin good moments and good relationships and good jobs. . . . I got to where I could not enjoy any happy moment without what felt like a dark frowning cloud hovering silently over it.*

A Bible study group that Amy attended happened to study the topic of how God binds up the broken-hearted. Amy concluded that even though she considered herself a Christian she certainly had not been living like one. She essentially was demonstrating that she had no faith in God whatsoever by always waiting for something bad to happen after a blessing.

While studying Scripture, Amy experienced an epiphany sparked by Isaiah 61: 1–3:

> *The spirit of the sovereign Lord is on me . . . He has sent me to comfort all who mourn, and provide for those who grieve in Zion—to bestow on them a crown of beauty instead of ashes, the oil of gladness instead of mourning, and a garment of praise instead of a spirit of despair.*

Amy concluded that this verse didn't mean she'll never mourn or feel despair. But Christ will joyfully minister His gladness on her once again. He will give her a heart of praise if she lets Him.

Amy not only switched to channel K-PRAY, she stayed tuned to her Christian station in great depth!

Two closing points: We need to be aware that it's very easy to switch from an affirmative channel back into a negative one out of habit. When you catch yourself doing so, just switch to a channel that's more supportive of the emotional state you desire.

And it's important to be kind to oneself when switching channels. When describing how to be gentle with your consciousness, there is a metaphor I like to use. Think of your mind as if it's a little boy on the Appalachian Trail whom you are following as well as guiding. As he wanders off to one side then to the other, as little ones are prone to do, you gently coach him back to the center of the trail. No scolding, just soft urging.

Letting go

Eli Mitchell & John Hoover

Eli: John, I'm struggling with an important psychotherapeutic, spiritual process that I call "Letting Go." It involves detaching with love, forgiveness, and moving on.

John: Why don't you pick out some themes that are a little more challenging than those? Just kidding.

Eli: I'd like to start out with one of my favorite Zen stories:

> *Two monks, one young, one old, were walking through the woods after a heavy rainstorm. Upon reaching a river that had almost gone over its banks, they saw a young and beautiful woman, dressed in an expensive silk robe, looking apprehensively at the water. Without a word, the older monk went to the lady, picked her up off her feet, and quickly carried her across the river. The younger monk hurried along after them. When they reached the other side, the beautiful woman gave the old monk a kiss on the cheek and went on her way. Through all this, the younger monk was silent. The two continued walking, the younger wanting to ask the elder about the woman, but kept his silence. After a while, he finally could not restrain himself and burst out, "We monks don't go near females, especially young and beautiful ones. Why did you carry her across?" "I put the woman down after we crossed the river," said the elder. "Why are you still carrying her?"*

John: I love that story, Eli. Just like the young monk, we can carry resentments for a long, long time. And mostly for the sneaky payoff our reactive mind gets: feeling righteous, superior, one-up. But the cost to us for getting that sneaky payoff is harmful to our physical, emotional, mental, and spiritual bodies, filling us with tension, rumination, depression, loss of joy, loss of integrity. The young monk's mind was preoccupied with disturbance, turmoil, ill-will . . . while the senior monk walks along with a mind free to experience stillness, peace, and contentment, because he let go of any mental attachments he might have had about breaking his vow by carrying the young woman across the river.

Eli: So true. So let's move on to the subject of detaching with love. When I am teaching clients about this process, I tell the following episode that occurred between my daughter and me.

After graduating from college, Tina was living in Florida and in the process of making a major life decision. The track she was on looked to me like an oncoming train wreck. When she came home every month or so, I figuratively waved my arms franticly trying to pressure her to change course. Of course, she did not respond favorably (at all) and insisted that since she is now an adult, she gets to make her own decisions.

John: Tina had you nailed with that one, didn't she?

Eli: Oh, yeah. So finally, after several of her visits home (all of which I was always able to make unpleasant with my lobbying), I decided it would be best to detach with love.

John: OK, how did you do that?

Eli: On her next visit, I apologized for pounding her for what I wanted her to do—or not to do. I told her she surely knew how I felt about the matter by now and that I would not broach the subject again unless she wanted to talk. Most importantly, I would accept and support whatever decision she made, and I would continue to love her unconditionally as best I could.

John: So you wisely bit the bullet . . . and your tongue!

Eli: Yes. Instead of our relationship continuing to go south, it returned to one of mutual respect and father-daughter love.

John: What an excellent resolution. Detachment with love is spot on. You let go of trying to control Tina . . . trying to get her to do what you wanted her to do. I know how you felt. As fathers we have been watchful, caring, and protective. We responsibly stepped in at times to place limits and give directions to our daughters. Sometimes it's challenging for us to know when to detach with love, that is, let go.

Eli: John, I have an epiphanic story about Lucy's "letting go of the past" that is dear to my heart.

John: Lay it on me.

Eli: Before Lucy and I were married, we dated for over two years. Both being in our mid-thirties we each had our baggage, of course, which came between us at times. This narrative is about how Lucy let go of a big, old "suitcase" on our wedding day.

Lucy's first marriage was to Tom, a man she met at the University of Michigan. After college, Tom went through flight school at the Naval Air Station in Pensacola, Florida. And he eventually served in Vietnam in the mid-1960s.

80

Phillip Craig, a good friend of Tom and Lucy's from college, also became a Navy pilot and flew F-4 jet missions in Nam. In a mission over North Vietnam a fellow pilot reported that he watched Phillip fly into a cloud bank, never to be seen again. Soon after, Phillip was listed as missing in action (MIA). Since more and more of the US military personnel became missing in action, a tradition began wherein family and friends wore a bracelet inscribed with the name of the missing service man and the date they were MIA. Typically, the bracelet was worn until the missing person's fate became known. The bracelets were designed to be slightly uncomfortable so as to remind the wearer of its purpose— "remember the one who is missing in action."

After Lucy learned that Phillip was MIA, she was grief stricken and prayed for him to be found alive and well. She decided that the least she could do would be to wear a bracelet as a reminder of her heroic friend Phillip and his plight.

When I met Lucy in 1975, she was still wearing this dedicated bracelet, and she continued to do so 24/7 during our two years of courtship. On a cloudy but pleasant day in May we were married in the mountains of East Tennessee in an outdoor ceremony. On our way to honeymooning in Gatlinburg a sudden thunderstorm pelted my truck with a spring rain. This downpour was strong enough to make me pull off the road. The storm ended as quickly as it began leaving an atmosphere of cleanliness, of refreshment, of newness. Looking at my beautiful new bride, it dawned on me that something else was amazingly new about Lucy. Her right wrist was bare—the bracelet was gone!

John: So Eli, Lucy was able to unpack her big old "suitcase" and air it out, and you both were able to move on from her past marriage relationship.

Eli: Yes. And years later, Lucy learned that Phillip's remains had been found in Vietnam and returned to his family in the United States. She sent the bracelet, along with a letter to Phillip's mother so she would have it for a special memorial service in his honor.

Debriefing the victims of 9-11

Eli Mitchell

Exactly a week before September 11, 2001, my daughter moved from her apartment in lower Manhattan back to Tennessee. Watching the World Trade Center disaster unfold on television at our home in Knoxville, my wife and I were stunned, horrified, and at the same time grateful that Tina was safe in Nashville.

> *Although the world is full of suffering, it is also full of the overcoming of it.*
>
> —Helen Keller

Since we had visited New York City several times each year during the five years Tina had lived there, and because we had joined the same international church as Tina, we knew many New Yorkers. About 100 of our church members were working in or near the World Trade Center on 9-11. Some were injured, though none were killed.

Being experienced in treating Posttraumatic Stress Disorder (PTSD) symptoms, and having been trained in Critical Incident Stress Debriefing and American Red Cross disaster mental health, I was eager ("Fit to be tied," according to my wife) to get to New York and see if I could help my fellow church members.

As I prepared for the long drive to Ground Zero, I called a crisis management company whose panel I was on and asked if they were enlisting debriefers for the World Trade Center disaster site. Not only did they retain me on the spot, they paid my expenses and put me up for ten nights in an excellent lower Manhattan hotel with some 70 other professionals.

Every morning we debriefers fanned out to different well-known businesses, both small and large, located in New York City or similar offices in New Jersey. Except for the loud, frenetic activity at Ground Zero, with wreckage piled several stories high, Manhattan was eerily subdued. The crowded, military-patrolled streets were hushed, conversations were few, and laughter was nonexistent. Cabbies were plentiful as always, but few kept the venerable practice of darting in-and-out of traffic while leaning on their horn.

The sobering fact that nobody had been found alive at Ground Zero since Wednesday, September 12th, the day after the attack, seemed to cast a pall over all of the flag-draped city.

Typically, our work assignment was to reinforce employee assistance program (EAP) personnel by debriefing company employees either in small groups or one-on-one sessions. We conducted "lunch and learn" groups focused on overcoming the symptoms of Acute Stress Disorder and on self-care and family wellness in the aftermath of a critical incident.

I learned an important lesson early on from my first one-on-one client. After we spent most of the hour processing her dramatic experience fleeing the North Tower of the World Trade Center, I asked, "What was the very worst part of the whole 9-11 disaster?" To my surprise, she said it was her constant dread of another attack. I then realized a terrorist incident is significantly different than other traumas I had treated. A natural disaster like a flood or hurricane, or even a violent personal assault like rape, is typically a one-time event for most people. On the other hand, a terrorist can hit the same target repeatedly and without warning. Hence, trauma symptoms like arousal and avoidance might be more intense after a disastrous incident created by terrorists.

From my experience with that first client, I also was made more aware that it was important to tell the truth as best I knew and not to be a Pollyanna about life when working with traumatized survivors. For example, I told my first client that I understood why she was anxious about the future and that the truth was we did not know if and when there would be more attacks—maybe, maybe not. The truth, however harsh, appeared to help the distressed victims I worked with to be more grounded.

In addition to debriefing company employees on weekdays for my crisis management company, during the evenings and over the one weekend I was there, I worked with members of my church by debriefing victims and educating them about psychological life shocks and the psytrauma recovery process.

One of the most poignant debriefing sessions I had was with a church member who was a female firefighter. For reasons of confidentiality, I'll call her Amy. On the morning of 9-11, a fellow firefighter asked Amy to change fire truck assignments with him. This was not an unusual request, so she readily agreed. His newly

> The Chinese have two characters for our word "crisis," one means danger and the other opportunity.
>
> –John F. Kennedy

assigned fire truck went out on the first 9-11 alarm to the World Trade Center. With the collapse of the South Tower that truck was crushed and no firefighters survived. Amy went out on the second alarm that morning and worked the disaster site without injury. For the next two weeks, every other shift for Amy and her peers involved grimly digging for possible survivors and human remains. Of course, her survivor guilt was tremendous.

Near the end of many one-on-one debriefing sessions, it felt right to ask, "Has anything good come out of all this trauma?" Every survivor I questioned responded positively. Silver linings abounded. There was the upwardly mobile executive with a wife and two kids who prided himself on 14-hour workdays. He now vowed to maintain a new schedule of much less work and "gobs more family time." Another executive, this one single, called himself a modern-day prodigal son. After 9-11 he began weekly visits to the New Jersey home of his previously estranged parents. A female employee became sort of a "prodigal mother" by tearfully reconciling with her long-lost daughter. Others pondered, "What is it all about?" and found their answer in a closer relationship with their Higher Power; they became more prayerful, read scripture, and went to synagogue, church, or other places of worship and meditation.

After ten full days of intense and rewarding trauma recovery work, I drove my rental car across lower Manhattan toward the Lincoln Tunnel heading south. Several cabbies blared their horns like the old days, protesting my Tennessee driving style—I gave them all thumbs up.

This essay was published in the *Vet Center Voice*, Vol. 23, No. 4.

The reframing of a tragedy

Eli Mitchell

The following is a true account of a local event that most of us would "frame" as a terrible tragedy. However, tt was superbly "reframed" by a Knoxville minister.

On Sunday morning, July 27, 2008, an unemployed ex-soldier opened fire with a 12-gauge shotgun inside the Tennessee Valley Universalist Unitarian Church (TVUUC) in West Knoxville during a children's play. The shooting stopped when several worshipers wrestled the gunman to the sanctuary floor. By then, one man lay dead, a woman was dying, and six others were wounded. Later the assailant said he wanted to kill as many liberals "where they gather" as he could and hoped to die in a shootout with police.

> The meaning that any event has depends upon the "frame" in which we perceive it. When we change the frame, we change the meaning.
>
> –Richard Bandler & John Grinder, *Reframing*

A week after the shooting the TVUUC held a sanctuary rededication ceremony which was televised and attended by an overflowing audience. The message delivered by Reverend Chris Buice proved to be a reframe of the recent trauma:

Last Sunday, a man walked into this sanctuary with the intention of inflicting terror, and he inspired quick and decisive acts of courage. . . . He came into this space with a desire to do an act of hatred, but he has unleashed unspeakable amounts of love. . . . A man tried to strike a blow for intolerance, and by so doing he inspired a gathering Monday night in the Second Presbyterian Church, and many other holy places throughout the week, a gathering of Christians and Jews, Muslims and Buddhists, believers and unbelievers, crowded in the aisles, sitting on the stage, standing outside in the rain, holding, hugging, and helping each other to heal. . . . A man tried to divide us, divide us into liberals and conservatives, gay and straight; instead his actions united us, making us more willing to listen to each other, care for each other, respect each other, support each other. . . . A man sought to alienate and isolate us, but our community surrounded us with love. . . . Our community is part of a larger world community, and we have many names for trying to describe that world community, and we are all of them today. We are God's children: red, yellow, black and white, gay and straight. We are all human, members of the human family, sharing one earth, sharing one common home. We are tied together, we are woven together, we are bound together in more ways than we can ever really know: . . . We Are One.

Exactly one year after the shooting, the TVUUC held an "Instruments of Peace" concert which was a "thank you" to police, emergency workers, disaster relief volunteers, and worshippers of all faiths who were supportive over the preceding twelve months. A large crowd gathered in the church sanctuary for a musical celebration of community solidarity, demonstrating the truth of Reverend Buice's reframe. More evidence of this truth is found in the fact that during the year after the attack, the TVUUC added some fifty members to their congregation. Also, two other local UUC churches similarly experienced growth and a renewed spirit as a result of the Knoxville community's response to the assault.

Since I was a Red Cross mental health volunteer for the church, I attended the concert celebration and afterwards was interviewed by a reporter and quoted in the next day's newspaper:

I've heard no bitterness and no desire for revenge but a lot of grace for all people . . . this experience came to be seen as an opportunity for spiritual growth and as an opportunity to reframe it—not as a tragedy, but as a time to make a leap forward in love.

The high power of ceremony

Eli Mitchell & Anonymous

Sometimes I ask a client to collaborate with me in writing up his or her therapeutic experience. In order to reinforce our work after a successful venture together, I might propose that we consolidate on paper our unique perspectives of the therapy. What follows is one of my favorite combined narratives. As you'll see, Dr. Ken B. is an excellent writer with quite a sense of humor.

Tuesday, February 13, 1994: Tossing down a small brown package on the desk, a pale and shaky Dr. Ken B. flopped into his usual seat in my psychotherapy office. In despair Ken explained that he had "relapsed, big-time." The package contained four vials of Demerol— leftovers from his death-defying weekend of drug mainlining.

> Ceremonial ritual, initiation rites, and ascetic practices, in all their forms and variations, interest me profoundly as so many techniques for bringing about a proper relation to these forces [of psychic life].
>
> –C. G. Jung, *The Collected Works, Vol. 4*

Ken sought me out some twenty months before in that great state of denial; according to Ken, the only problem was depression, not his alcoholic behavior or his illegal biweekly binges abusing narcotics. He had been a highly successful surgeon. Three years into his professional practice he started the "recreational" use of Demerol. By the time Ken first entered my office, six years later, he had a full-blown addiction. In the previous month he had voluntarily stopped performing surgery; the day following our first session, Ken closed down his office.

After several sessions of gentle persuasion, Ken reluctantly agreed to a short inpatient stay for an assessment of his "depression." He entered an alcohol and drug treatment center in a nearby city. Ken writes:

Somehow my five-day evaluation blossomed into a four month inpatient and halfway house experience. My new title, formerly and exclusively "Doctor," was now "drug addict and alcoholic." My actions were reminiscent of a sputtering A-Model on a cold morning. I didn't quit (trying to recover), and neither could I get moving down that long road (toward quality sobriety).

During my stay, I managed to dodge mainstream recovery and complete involvement with the ceremonial rituals of the Twelve-Step Program. This program embraces first, the humbling aspects of admission and submission, but second and very important to me, is the element of celebration.

Yes, I applauded those who "surrendered" and took a white chip to symbolize the beginning of sobriety, and some who received 30- and 60-day chips. And, yes, I desired the gifts that come with sobriety and recovery. However, I was not convinced that I really wanted to live drug-free—or even could. As long as these questions persisted in my mind, I knew I was apt to relapse. There were many patients with a collection of white chips which to me represented failed commitments. I saw no benefit in taking a white chip unless I was truly committed.

Consequently, all the while I was involved with the treatment program, I never took a white chip to mark a date of total surrender. I was even so self-defeatingly clever to fool the program's vigilant urine-monitoring system. (Beneath my armpit I rigged up an IV fluid bag filled with "clean" urine and ran the tubing under my clothing to the end of my penis. While in front of the male staff monitor, I was able to compress the bag under my arm and, undetected, I delivered untainted tinkle. I managed to graduate from treatment with my usual A in appearance and F in inner peace.

After treatment center discharge, Ken returned home and worked hard in semi-weekly psychotherapy. We focused primarily on his deep shame issues passed on by rigid, fundamentalist parenting. Often Ken grappled tearfully with his old, tenacious belief that he was "less than" everybody else. His early experiences had been just that; he wore permanent eyeglasses by age two and corrective shoes for a diagnosed foot deformity. Lacking in coordination and any semblance of confidence, Ken was an underachiever all through his elementary and high school years.

In spite of his intensive psychotherapy and daily twelve-step meetings, for four months after treatment center graduation Ken continued to abuse narcotics and sometimes marijuana, binging several times monthly. Then he was able to "stiff-arm" addictive substances and became free of drugs and alcohol for the next four months. However, the temptations around Christmas time proved to be too challenging,

> Rarely have we seen a person fail who has thoroughly followed our path. Those who do not recover are people who cannot or will not completely give themselves to this simple program.
>
> –Alcoholic Anonymous,
> Third Edition

and Ken had a major five-day Demerol relapse. Some six weeks later he finally hit bottom:

Growing disgust with myself led me to make the largest narcotic order I had ever dared risk. I had previously used caution so as not to red-flag the Drug Enforcement Agency. This time I cared little. From the moment I placed the order, until its arrival five days later, I trembled with anticipation. Cost me over $600 to repair the fellow's car I blatantly ran into at the UPS parking lot.

Jitters? Not me. I had already set up my little MASH unit at home with new butterfly needles, alcohol wipes, tape neatly torn into strips to hold the IVs in place, syringes readied, the TV remote in place, food, water, and all the essentials. Few brides have their wedding chambers as completely prepared. All that was lacking was the bride. I carried her over the threshold Friday afternoon.

Several days later I awakened in my disheveled bed, bloated, filthy, and covered with scattered traces of dried blood. A butterfly needle hung from my left arm with the cap and syringe missing. The blood from my arm had flowed backwards, dripping out of the open tubing onto the pillow, across the edge of the mattress and ultimately pooling on the floor. My arm was swollen and an obvious hematoma had formed. I vaguely remember opening my eyes to this and chuckling at my dilemma, "How absurd you are. Did you enjoy your trip? I don't remember any trip. And three-fourths of a drug order that should last two years in my practice—gone in just . . . What day is it?"

Monday, February 12th. Lethargically I cleaned up the mess, aired out the stench in the room, and awaited the freezing sweats. As I bagged what little narcotic was left, I toyed with the idea of turning it over to Eli (Dr. Mitchell). What if I changed my mind later? No, if I'm going to be "rigorously" honest and tell him, I better take him a sign of good faith. OK then, how about taking him just one of the bottles? Nope, go all the way. Give it up.

Tuesday, February 13th, I entered "The Big Sponge" (my affectionate title for Eli's office because of the flood of tears shed there), and I handed over the leftover narcotics. Yeah, yeah, I cried and admitted I was powerless and all that. Then I demanded, "What's the prescription, Doc? Fix me or at least tell me where you get the cure."

"Ken, are you working the twelve-step program?"

"Sure, I'm working my program. I'm saturated with meetings, reading, and all that stuff."

"But are you working THE program?"

"Well, I haven't really done everything. I've never taken chips and, uh, maybe I don't pray enough . . . uh . . ."

Silence. I find these brief periods of silence a ploy designed to allow the therapist to nap and the patient time to thrash about in his own muck.

Back awake, Eli probed, "Do you have a sponsor?"

"Well, yes, well, no, well I've tried and they're busy, well . . ."

Muck again.

THE program, huh. Thy will, not my will, be done. Ceremonial meetings with readings from the A.A. Big Book. Walking the walk of the twelve steps. Sponsors. Promises. An opening ritual of the Serenity Prayer ("God, grant me the serenity to accept the things I cannot change . . ."), a closing with the "chip system" and the Lord's Prayer. "Keep coming back. It works if you work it."

My usual hide-out was twelve-step meetings in the inner city. There no one knew me and

> Ritual and ceremony in general are ways of using small, symbolic acts to set up a connection between the conscious mind and the unconscious.
>
> —Robert Johnson, *Inner Work*

didn't bother to try. Of course, arriving late and leaving early made it a little tough for anybody to even get acquainted with me. I wasn't good at sharing my hope, didn't care to share my experience, and I had no strength. Sharing of experience, strength, and hope, humph, another damn ceremony. I sincerely believed that as much as I wanted sobriety, I could make it happen. The truth was that after giving it my best for well over a year, it was not happening.

Wednesday, February 14th. Well maybe the trick to this sobriety thing is to work THE program, not MY program. I arrived at an inner city meeting, shaking and still clammy. Tearfully and with humility, I shared the story of my relapse and told my history of chip rejection. For the first time, I took a white chip. It felt good. Love in a plastic poker chip. Later, I bored a hole in it and pinned it to my wall. It's a piece of me.

I stored away Ken's package of Demerol along with the issue of how to handle this "gift." Occasionally I would ponder what to do about the stash. Following suggestions from a colleague, I finally knew what direction to take when the time was right. In the meantime, Ken continued to struggle productively in therapy. He never mentioned his drugs in my possession.

Those weeks after the turn over of the Demerol to Eli were marked by fantasies that occur to few but the insanely addicted. My actions stayed clean and sober, but as they say in A.A., my thinking stunk. I imagined breaking and entering his office to search for the drugs. I often questioned myself as to whether or not he really still had the stuff. I wondered if Eli might try the narcotic himself to see if he liked it. (That's what I would have done!) Surely he'll have the drug on file under my name and there it will be. I'll withdraw the Demerol with a syringe and refill the bottles with water; he would never know. And on, and on, and on. . . .

Occasionally, Eli throws me a ringer. This particular day it came near the end of a therapeutic session which had been basically upbeat. I've learned to tread cautiously when I hear; "Ken, I'd like to try something new with you." It usually means another sponge-soaker. Anyway, I always attempt to be willing so as to get my money's worth. But can you believe this? He wants me to pour the contents of the narcotic bottles into his toilet!

This request jolted me. What's he doing? Non-electrical shock therapy? Doesn't he know I'm a drug addict? Divorcing the bride is hard enough without this! I cried and squirmed. "Where's that coming from?" Eli asked. I really, really didn't know. It was like an orthopedic surgeon putting his stiff thumb into a ruptured disc and asking, "Does this hurt?" "Yes, it hurts." "Why?" "'Cause you've got your thumb in it."

I just couldn't do it that day. We studied the calendar and August 14th, several weeks away, looked better. That was my 40th birthday, several days before my trip to Canada, and

> Doing a physical act has a magical effect on dream work. It takes your understanding of the dream off the purely abstract level and gives it an immediate concrete reality . . . Rituals provide us a way of taking principals from the unconscious and impressing them vividly on the conscious mind. But rituals also have an effect on the unconscious. A highly conscious ritual sends a powerful message back to the unconscious, causing changes to take place at the deep levels where our attitudes and values originate.
>
> —Robert Johnson, *Inner Work*

most importantly, it marked six months of being clean and sober.

For the next weeks, rarely a day went by that I didn't think about the scenario of pouring out the Demerol. I played scenes over and over in my mind. Would I open it? Would he? The office bathroom seemed like the wrong place to do it. Not at all appropriate. Cramped for two people, too small for a ceremony, and besides I occasionally have to use that thing.

The evening before the BIG DAY, I prayed and had my own ceremony of gratitude. I was real thankful for six months of being free from alcohol and drugs. Before accepting the white chip, I had not been able to achieve nearly this length of clean time. Truly a gift.

The next morning I awoke quite early, prayed again, dosed back off to sleep, and dreamed of my journey to Eli's office.

I entered the room where we meet which now overlooked a lake with towering slopes on the opposite bank. A feeling of peace filled me; a peace with the kind of joy that only comes with quiet gratitude. An open porch outside the office protruded over the water. Eli and I went outside, planning to pour the Demerol into the water. It started to pour, and Eli said, "Wait, this thing floats." He detached the deck from the bank and we floated down the lake to our right. The experience of pouring out the drugs was shared between us. Then I wanted to throw the empty bottles into the lake. I hesitated out of my concern that Eli would think it "an unsound ecological practice." My tension about ecology soon faded and was replaced by a strong sense of freedom. As the dream ended, a breeze caressed my face. . . .

Immediately upon my actual arrival at Eli's office I shared this dream—hot off the press. I enjoy Eli's "natural child" as he frequently allows to surface. "Let's do it!" popped out this time, "I know just the place." He grabbed the Demerol package and we both headed for the door.

We drove to the bank of a large lake nearby, and as we approached a parking area, Eli's kid showed up again. "Looka' there . . . wild Canada Geese!" Neither one of us had ever seen wild geese on the banks within this residential area. Not one or two, but an entire flock! "Do you know what that means?" Eli asked. Then he answered, "They're symbolic of the Holy Spirit." Now I know what it feels like to have the hair on one's back and neck stand straight up. A tingling traveled down my spine and radiated to my fingertips. I felt like stopping as if this Holy Place shouldn't be entered. Eli's enthusiasm overtook my hesitancy. We parked near a huge oak tree and stepped into the mild, mid-day summer sun.

I felt I had no control over any of this and could hardly speak. I was very uncertain as to what to do. In need of direction, I looked to Eli to initiate this unique ceremony.

"Pick a spot," Eli said, matter of factly. Pick a spot? Just a spot? The nearby lake glistened from sunlight, but my sensation was that of walking into a strange dark room, groping for the light switch, and fearing something precious might be knocked over and broken.

At lake's edge I nervously pried off the metal and rubber cap of the first vial of Demerol with a screwdriver; then the remaining three bottles, each with more and more assurance. Some of the "liquid hell" spilled on my fingers but it had no power. In the past there was great excitement when in contract with this stuff. Not now. Holding the full bottles evoked nothing in my soul.

Like the dream, Eli and I took turns pouring out the narcotic into the water which drifted right. (Later, I learned left-to-right movement in a dream might symbolize forward progress, a moving on.) As the clear Demerol dissipated in the lake, I sensed no difference between it and the water into which it was poured. No feeling of fear. No sense of regret or loss. The shaking hands that previously held the full bottles of narcotics no longer shook.

"You're free!" Eli whooped, and we slung the bottles, singing through the air, far into the lake. We embraced. The breeze was slight and just enough to bathe me in feelings of freedom.

We talked and strolled along the bank toward the wild geese. Eli tried to get in rapport with one of them by mimicking the erect posture and jerky movements of the goose's head with his arm and hand. (He's crazy . . . but I won't tell.)

Indeed I felt the presence of the Holy Spirit. As we observed the flock pecking for food in the field, there were two geese that did not feed but watched carefully over the others. I felt then and often feel this way now: a sense of freedom while Someone watches over me.

Thank God for miracles!

Ken's courageous miracle of recovery took place over sixteen years ago. Since then, our paths cross every year or so. I'm happy to report that Ken has remained clean and sober all this time. I talked with him last month and learned that he is now a successful realtor (even in these hard economic times). Ken said he enjoys his work and his parting comment was, "I can't and don't complain; life is right good."

OUR PERSONAL PATHS

Shedding the "nice boy" drama

Eli Mitchell

Mom had been bedridden at home for months suffering from an enlarged heart caused by Rheumatic Fever. Three weeks after my sixth birthday, I walked into her bedroom, saw her empty bed, and knew something was terribly wrong. Overwhelmed, I couldn't hear what the adults in the room were saying. However, later that morning, I was taken for a ride in a convertible by a woman in the neighborhood that I didn't know very well. During this ride, my neighbor seemed to be telling me, "Don't feel sad about the death of your mother, just enjoy the ride." I bought into that injunction, and I didn't grieve until many years later.

After this heart-breaking blow, I evidently decided: "If I get close to somebody they will die." Furthermore, I remember that many times as a child I would crawl on my mother's bed to be beside her only to be told by an adult to get down because my mother needed to rest. This repeated scene probably led me to draw an even more dramatic conclusion: "My love kills."

Soon after my mother died, I began acting out a specific drama— the "nice boy." I began following a script that probably developed naturally out of my passive demeanor: "I'm a nice, quiet, motherless little boy, so I need you to take care of me." This script initially worked like a charm, especially with several mothers of my friends in the neighborhood. During this time, I don't remember ever throwing a temper tantrum, and my mood was typically dysthymic, a mood disorder characterized by chronic mild depression and despondency.

Overbrook Circle where we lived was a close-knit, middle class neighborhood of seven families whose backyards shared mutual boundaries and gravel alleyways. Three other boys lived on Overbrook Circle, and their mothers bought into my script (thank God) and took turns mothering me to different degrees.

Every day of grammar school, Hugh's lovely mom drove him and me to school. In the morning I would walk through our backyards and typically would arrive at my best friend's back door as Hugh and his little sister were finishing up breakfast. His mother inevitability would ask if I would like some breakfast, and I inevitability lied and said, "No thank you, I've already eaten." Besides rides to school, Hugh's family took me on various outings and to special events. Most exciting was when we drove out into the countryside every Fourth of July, and under close parental supervision, Hugh and I shot off fireworks for hours. In summertime another neighborhood family, whose son "Tex" was my buddy, took me to their lake place to picnic, fish, and swim.

My script worked its magic all during grammar school. In my early teens however, I was smart enough (subconsciously) to drop the motherless, little boy drama but kept the nice, people-pleasing mask.

Greenville (South Carolina) Junior and Senior High Schools were quite social as well as educational institutions. At the end of the seventh grade, most of us were "rushed" by five different clubs and some of us would be chosen to join. These clubs had very different memberships. One was populated by preppy boys from wealthy families while another was composed of rougher, hell-raising types.

Rushed by all five of these varied groups, I got a bid to join each one of them. I was delighted. WOW, how popular can one get! Looking back, I see that I was the perfect chameleon; I could match any color of any group with ease. Also, I see now that the cost to my true self was high.

Later on in college, my phony, people-pleasing scenario devolved into playing the fraternity dummy. With chagrin, I recall my nickname in those days: "Wedge"—the simplest of all tools. Ouch.

While I was earning a Ph.D. in Clinical Psychology, after having been a Navy officer for three years, I even undercut my personal power by telling some family and friends at home that I was studying to be a child psychologist, implying that I wasn't quite up to working with adults.

As I evolved from being a grad student into becoming "Dr. Mitchell," I noticed on occasion I would be a nervous authority figure when around other authority figures! Yes, even at 69-years-old with over 36 years of experience as a therapist, I still have to overcome occasional twinges of feeling like that six-year-old who just lost his mother.

It took years just to get a good handle on the trauma of my mother's death along with the drama and the beliefs it precipitated. My personal therapy journey really started in 1970 when I trained at the Gestalt Therapy Institute of Los Angeles. I had group sessions with several inspiring psychotherapists who were trained and certified by Fritz Perls, the founder of Gestalt therapy, including Eric Marcus, M.D. and Bob Resnick, Ph.D., author of *Chicken Soup Is Poison*.

The format in which our training took place was essentially one-on-one individual psychotherapy within a group setting. Taking the "hot seat" in the middle of the group of 15 trainees, I told the trainer I wanted to work on my problem of wanting everybody to like me. He directed me to go around the group, look at one person at a time, and tell each individual how vital it was that they liked me. By the time I got to the fifth person, it dawned on me that I was way overstating the case. It certainly wasn't vital that everyone of them like me. As I continued to make my round, I became more and more aware (and I told them so) that for some of them I preferred that they liked me, and for some it mattered a little, and for others I really didn't care one way or the other!

When I pictured the whole group in my mind's eye, I really wanted all of them to like me, but when I was instructed to be in the now by going person-to-person, face-to-face, I realized my true feelings. It mattered that some people liked me, but certainly not everyone. I gave away my power when I thought in the abstract about the group, but when I was grounded in the now and speaking directly to each individual, I became aware of my real stance.

My long-over-due post-traumatic healing continued with a nine-month Gestalt training program in Atlanta led by Joen Fagan and Irma Lee Shepherd, two extraordinary therapists who had also been trained in Gestalt therapy by Dr. Perls. Through the process of Redecision Therapy, I was able to transform that unhealthy belief into a relationship-affirming stance.

I was led through a process in which I recreated the scenes from my childhood in which I made false decisions—"I have to be a nice boy," "my love kills," et cetera. With guidance from the therapist, I experienced the child part of myself and emotionally re-decided and chose life-affirming beliefs that were true, such as "I can just be me" and "I can love without fear of being abandoned."

A year after I completed Gestalt training and the healing process associated with it, I was able to enter into a healthy relationship for the first time. I started dating Lucy, and after a two-year courtship, we married. We've been spasmodically happily married for over 33 years.

The Buckdancer

One of my favorite nice boy "wake-up call" events happened some twenty years ago. On an afternoon in the middle of my work week, I began to feel out of gas, called it a day, and went home several hours early. Sitting on the side of my bed, right before crashing, a voice (thankfully, inside my head) said, "Eli, you're a buck dancer." That's all. I took notice because an inside voice had never addressed me before in the third person. Being perplexed, I wondered "What's that about?"

A few days later I got it. What came to mind was a book of poetry by James Dickey, *Buckdancer's Choice*, in which the title poem speaks of the minstrel show *Bucks* wherein African-American men performed shuffle and tap dance routines in the late 19th century. I realized the voice was telling me that I was like them—whenever a tune (i.e. an invitation to speak) came along with a captive audience, I was out there just a' dancin'!

Soon after this insight, I was invited to give a talk to a church audience. I readily declined. On an earlier date, I would have accepted even though I might not have known much about the topic. I had became much more selective about what tunes to which I chose to dance.

Learning to ride the horse in the direction that the horse is going

John Hoover

Back in my high school days, I had the attitude of a passive-aggressively defiant victim, with no intention of ever going on to any kind of schooling. Yet wanting to "get out of Dodge," I defaulted to military service. My friend Jim Gamber persuaded me to go with him to the Marine Corps Reserve meetings during my senior year. A month after graduating from high school, we were off to Parris Island to begin three years of active duty in the Marine Corps.

The legendary boot camp training at Parris Island is a challenge for any recruit who has ever matriculated the thirteen week indoctrination. The physical demands pale in comparison to the structure of discipline imposed on the recruits every minute of your time on the Island. The Semper Fi fraternity of Drill Instructors (DIs) takes over your mind, body, and soul in a way that even other military services can't imagine. The DIs demand your absolute compliance from the moment you are awakened in the morning with their screaming, and yelling "Get out of the rack, you maggots! Get out, get out, get out!" to the command of "Lights out; evening prayers" at night.

I knew how to be totally compliant and obedient to authority and not even entertain defiant thoughts in my mind; just be invisible and do what I was told. It was several months after boot camp that defiance rose up in me big time.

After boot camp at Parris Island, all of us proceeded on to Infantry Training Regiment (ITR) at Camp LeJeune, North Carolina. All Marines are trained first to be basic infantrymen. In the weeks at ITR we were taught the tactics and strategies of fighting in combat. We were introduced to all different kinds of weaponry and maneuvers. We were no longer recruits; we were Marines.

After ITR, I was sent to a specialty school for four months at the Naval Base in Norfolk, Virginia, to learn International Morse Code and become a radio telegrapher. I did pretty well at finals, sending 28 words per minute and receiving 32 words per minute. I also took up boxing and was trained by one of the members of the All-Navy Boxing Team. That was fun until he showed me first-hand how much of a beginner I really was. He could punch really hard when he wanted to!

My defiant attitude came out full blown in the company to which I was assigned after radio school: 2nd Anglico (Air and Naval Gunfire Liaison Company). In 2nd Anglico, I was recreating my whole high school demeanor but now with hostility. To say that I had a chip on my shoulder about life would be putting it mildly. I exhibited passive defiance of any authority. And there I was in the Marine Corps!

Each day we would be assigned tasks to do to clean up the barracks before going to the practice maneuvers in the field. No matter what my assignment was, I would do it with such grumbling, cussing, and resistance as to make things messier. I recall a time when Corporal Higgins, just looked at me, shook his head, and said, "Hoover, you cuss harder than anybody that I have ever known." I had a notoriously foul mouth that was even offensive to Marines and Sailors! At an evaluation by the senior NCOs of my company, Staff Sergeant Sutherland and Sergeant Humbert encouraged me to transfer to some other company, advising that I would never make any promotions if I stayed in this company. I stayed, defiantly.

But something happened somewhere along the way. I woke up one morning while I was aboard a Navy troop transport ship as part of a battalion of Marines maintaining a combat-ready presence in the Mediterranean Ocean. We had been out to sea for two or three months. My company, 2nd Anglico, was quartered in the forward compartment of the USS Fremont that morning I woke up. I got out of my rack, and it was as if I had truly awakened. It was as if I were seeing the world in a way that I had not seen it before, and I was seeing my relationship with that world.

There is a Chinese proverb that goes something like, "It is best to ride the horse in the direction that the horse is going." I saw metaphorically that I had been sitting on a horse facing its tail and was mad as hell that I didn't have any control of where things were going. I immediately saw that I had been a victim of my own making. And I saw all that with great compassion and excitement.

I don't even know why I did what I did next. I opened my foot locker, pulled out a 3" x 5" card, and wrote on it, "Please do not take the Lord's name in vain, He's a friend of mine." And I scotch taped it to the chain that holds up the outside of the rack, that I slept on. The next thing I did was go to the ship's library, a small, rarely-used room on the ship. I vividly remember sitting at the table in that library looking at the few hundred books shelved there and feeling thrilled with the notion that all these smart people have put their thoughts and ideas into these books, and all I have to do is read them and I can have their smarts. It was right then and there that I made a decision to go to college. I left the ship's library and walked into a new world.

I enrolled in correspondence courses within the next week. In the next evaluation by the company senior NCOs I received a commendation for outstanding Marine of the company. It was all just easy. I just rode the horse in the direction that the horse was going. I felt no resistance, no ill-will towards authority or their assignments. I saw that whatever there was to do, I could do with or without resistance, and it was a lot easier to just do it. I enjoyed the energy that was not being expended in the form of againstness.

I felt a huge relief. My resistance had been like a prison keeping the real me from participating constructively in life.

I went to college after leaving my tour of duty in the Marine Corps and kept riding the horse, even began using the reins. I had a new life. I stopped being invisible. In my freshman year in college, I was elected president of my freshman class, elected to student court, student council, was named representative student, played varsity football, sang in the a cappella choir, and I studied more than any other human being that I have ever known.

I became determined to succeed in the classroom. I still had all that past school experience of doing poorly and believing I wasn't college material. I was scared I would fail. However, I knew that what I was bringing to the table was a great deal of willingness and self-discipline. The Marine Corps equipped me with discipline, and I internalized that discipline. And somehow through it all, I created my own strategy for overcoming the obstacles that dyslexia and ADD naturally present to anyone's ability to learn in the typical classroom.

I think every moment along our path of life, life is capable of waking us up to new possibilities, new choices, to live in greater harmony with all other beings, to riding the horse in the direction it's going. The question is: "Do we say 'yes' to life's wakeup calls?"

A personal story of recovery

Eli Mitchell

In the fall of 1985, several weeks before a Halloween alcohol blackout shattered my fortress of denial, Lucy had—what I called—"blown my cover" by attending Al-Anon meetings. Here I was, a respected clinical psychologist in the community and, since I didn't understand that "Anon" really did mean anonymous, I thought she was announcing my alleged alcoholism not only to the local community, but to the entire Southeast. Then I worried that somehow word would get out to the Americas followed by announcements to the whole Western world.

Bowing to the terror of having experienced an emotionally devastating blackout, to shame, and to Lucy's loving but adamant stance, I reluctantly asked a friend with years in the program to take me to an Alcoholics Anonymous meeting. Once across the threshold of that church basement, I realized that this was where I belonged: surrounded by a group of twenty-or-so caring men who, on my behalf, returned to Step One of the Big Book of Alcoholics Anonymous and shared stories admitting they "were powerless over alcohol" and that their "lives had become unmanageable." They contended that unless we are totally surrendered, the program will not work: "Almost surrendering is like almost having a parachute."

When I finally began the process of "turning it over" to a Power greater than myself at that first AA meeting, by the grace of God I had a humbling but relatively high "bottom."

This means that I was not devastated like many recovering alcoholics are initially: I didn't lose my wife and daughter (just my self-respect for awhile), nor my friends, nor my career, nor did I physically injure myself or anybody else.

We recovering alcoholics never fully "recover" because the struggle with our addiction, to different degrees, is always ongoing. "One day at a time." For several years I attended AA meetings regularly and "with a little help from my friends" and family, I moved on from stiff-arming alcohol to a loss of desire to drink. Working and reworking the Twelve Steps since that first meeting has been foundational to my emotional, interpersonal, and spiritual growth.

Steps Four and Five were pivotal for me. Step Four states that we have "made a searching and fearless moral inventory of ourselves." During this process of honest and rigorous self-examination, I took stock of my character defects—"sins" in Christian terms—such as being selfish, deceptive, and unforgiving, to name a few. Also, an egoism housecleaning was essential in order to deal with both my inflated ego (prideful) and a deflated ego (resentful).

Resentment is the "number one" offender. It destroys more alcoholics than anything else. From it stem all forms of spiritual disease, for we have been not only mentally and physically ill, we have been spiritually sick. When the spiritual malady is overcome, we straighten out mentally and physically.

In Step Five we "admitted to God, to ourselves, and to another human being the exact nature of our wrongs." This Step is a way of taking ownership of all of our shortcomings generated in the moral inventory. Fortunately a Catholic priest (who was in recovery also) was available to be my "another human being" and my quasi-religious confession turned out to be extremely freeing.

> **The Serenity Prayer**
>
> *God grant me the serenity to accept the things I cannot change;*
>
> *The courage to change the things I can; and wisdom to know the difference.*
>
> *Living one day at a time;*
>
> *Enjoying one moment at a time;*
>
> *Accepting hardships as the pathway to peace;*
>
> *Taking, as He did, this sinful world as it is, not as I would have it;*
>
> *Trusting that He will make all things right if I surrender to His Will;*
>
> *That I may be reasonably happy in this life and supremely happy with Him forever in the next.*
>
> —Reinhold Niebuhr

I worked the Twelve Steps unremittingly, and now, thanks to the Creator, I can gratefully say I've been a recovering alcoholic for over twenty-four years.

The Twelve Steps and their Biblical comparisons

From a Knoxville Celebrate Recovery Ministry pamphlet. Biblical comparisons are in italics.

1) We admitted we were powerless over our addictions and compulsive behaviors. That our lives had become unmanageable. *For I know that nothing good lives in me, that is, in my sinful nature. For I have the desire to do what is good, but I cannot carry it out.* (Romans 7:18)

2) Came to believe that a power greater than ourselves could restore us to sanity. *For it is God who is at work in you, both to will and to act according to His good purpose.* (Philippians 2:13)

3) Made a decision to turn our will and our lives over to the care of God. *I urge you, therefore, brothers and sisters, in view of God's great mercy, to offer yourselves as living sacrifices, holy and pleasing to God—this is your spiritual act of worship.* (Romans 12:1)

4) Made a searching and fearless moral inventory of ourselves. *Let us examine our ways and test them, and let us return to the LORD.* (Lamentations 3:40)

5) Admitted to God, to ourselves, and to another human being, the exact nature of our wrongs. *Therefore, confess your sins to each other, and pray for each other, so that you may be healed.* (James 5:16a)

6) Were entirely ready to have God remove all these defects of character. *Humble yourselves before the Lord, and he will lift you up.* (James 4:10)

7) Humbly asked Him to remove all our shortcomings. *If we confess our sins, He is faithful and just and will forgive us our sins and purify us from all unrighteousness.* (1 John 1:9)

8) Made a list of all persons we had harmed and became willing to make amends to them all. *Do to others, as you would have them do to you.* (Luke 6:31)

9) Made direct amends to such people whenever possible, except when to do so would injure them or others. *Therefore, if you are offering your gift at the altar, and there remember that someone has something against you, leave your offering there in front of the altar. First go and be reconciled to your brother or sister, and then come and offer your gift.* (Matthew 5:23-24)

10) Continued to take personal inventory and when we were wrong, promptly admitted it. *So, if you think you are standing firm, be careful that you don't fall.* (1 Corinthians 10:12)

11) Sought through prayer and meditation to improve our conscious contact with God, praying only for knowledge of His will for us and power to carry that out. *Let the word of Christ dwell in you daily.* (Colossians 3:16)

12) Having had a spiritual experience as the result of these steps, we tried to carry this message to others, and practice these principles in all our affairs. *Brothers and sisters, if a man is caught in a sin, you who are spiritual should restore him gently. But watch yourself, or you also may be tempted.* (Galatians 6:1)

The life jolt

Eli Mitchell & John Hoover

Eli: John, let's swap "life jolts" . . . those past pleasurable, emotional experiences that lead to life-giving beliefs about self, others, and the world we know.

John: So, you're talking about experiences that flashback in our memories with vivid images, stereophonic sound, heightened emotions, strong physical sensations, even smells and tastes?

OK, I've got a good, recent life jolt that occurred earlier this spring in South Africa. Sharon and I went to the bush in Zulu territory for three days with two couples who live in Durban, South Africa. We stayed in cabins in the wild. Zulu staff people prepared our food. Two guides armed with high powered rifles took us into the bush for three-hour hikes each morning to see the wild animals living in their natural habitat. On the drive from Durban to the iMfolozi reserve, I shared with A.J. and his wife, Wendy, that a number of years earlier I had done a Shamanic journey and believed I had met my *power animal*, a Cape Buffalo.

A.J. and Wendy speak several African languages including Zulu. After speaking with the Zulu staff about my Shamanic experience, A.J. told me that the Zulus agreed that "Inyathi" ("buffalo" in Zulu) was my spirit animal. Thereafter all the Zulu staff addressed me only as Inyathi. They would greet me with big smiles, eyes open very wide, shake my hand in their particular Zulu handshake, and nodding their heads speak with such nobility the words: "Inyathi!" "Inyathi!" I loved it.

Eli: Outstanding, John . . . I mean Inyathi. That sounds inspiring.

A wonderful life jolt whacked me when I was seven years old. I received the unexpected Christmas gift of a microscope. While visiting over the holidays, my cousin, a biology major in college, coached me in simply putting two drops of water from a potted plant on a slide. When I viewed this water through the scope, a whole new, fascinating, unforgettable world of protozoa opened up for me: amoebas, paramecium cells swimming with their numerous cilia, and so on. This universe I never knew was literally right under my nose! I was amazed at the thought that there must be so much more in life to discover and explore than I had ever imagined.

John: . . . a whole new relationship to reality, so to speak, that there's more than what meets the eye, can virtually mean opening up to new realms of existence that one never even considered before. That event was really a great jolt.

Eli: You know, in the same way that events can create a life jolt, so can "one liners" if spoken by a person of influence in our lives.

I remember it well: When I was a senior in college trying to decide on a career path, I told a psychology professor I worked for that I was considering getting a masters degree to teach history in high school. The professor's casual remark, "You can go further than that" resonated so well and deep that, years later, I earned a Ph.D. in psychology.

John: Yea for your psych professor!

How I snapped out of a depression

Eli Mitchell

Paula, a black-haired, beautiful woman of Italian ancestry, married my fraternity brother, Don; I had the pleasure of being his best man. A few months into their marriage, Paula began developing multiple sclerosis. As you may know, MS commits chronic, progressive thievery by stealing many neurological and cognitive functions, piece by piece, year by year.

I visited Paula over the Christmas season of 1982, eight years into her illness. She was perky and gracious, a queen, holding court from her king-size bed. During my visit she would not allow any discussion of her condition. She brushed off any focus on herself or her debilitating illness. She could not walk, read, or write. However, Paula remained a better wife and mother than most, albeit mostly from her bed. Her phone calling neuro-anatomy was a "go," and she networked for hours every day on her phone with other victims of MS, mainly as their counselor, being the wounded healer that she is.

As I left, Paula mentioned she had been interviewed by a reporter from *Ladies Home Journal.* An article would be out spring or summer in the coming year.

Several months later, beset by a "poor me" depression, I was barely getting through my morning psychotherapy sessions. During lunch break, I walked to an old-fashioned drugstore down the street from my office and sat down at the counter to eat. Midway through my grilled cheese sandwich, I remembered what Paula had said about her magazine interview and thought maybe her story would be in the latest *Journal.* I browsed the magazine rack—sure enough there it was! Sitting at the counter again, engrossed, these sentences popped off the page:

> *During those first three months I used to lie in bed and think, "Oh, if I could just get to the kitchen . . . if I could have just one meal with my family." I thought it was all I would ever want out of life. And then one day I did get down the stairs, and I'll never forget it! I sat down on the bottom step, and thought about how beautiful the kitchen looked with the sun streaming in. Even the plants I'd hung looked greener than I'd remembered them. I sat there in rapture.*

I became awakened to reality the moment I began reading that article. What was I thinking? Snap out of it, man!

It was obvious that Paula perceived her circumstances in a way that didn't bring her down into depression or self-pity. And I knew how to do that! I can perceive even difficult things as they are without going into self-pity or victimhood. Just like that, I shifted to that perspective. Bingo, I was free!

Immediately I felt an abundance of energy and a strong sense of gratitude.

I sprinted back to my office, canceled my remaining clients of the day, went home and grabbed Buddy, my golden retriever, and happily jogged three miles in the warm spring afternoon sunshine.

You can play the game hurt, but not injured.

John Hoover

Since football is such a rough sport, it makes sense to play the game in such a way as to not get injured. All the players wear pads to keep from getting injured. But to play the game so as to not get hurt . . . well, that just doesn't fit for the game of football.

Unfortunately, when I went out for football in my junior year in high school I didn't understand the distinction between playing to not get hurt and playing to not get injured. To me they meant the same thing. Get a picture of that. There I was, wanting to play football and afraid of getting hurt. You can imagine what that looks like . . . then go ahead and imagine how much time I spent on the bench watching high school football games rather than participating!

But what I've since realized is that this is not really a story about football; it's a story about life. We want to play the life game, but we are often afraid of getting hurt . . . or worse. People often don't understand that taking risks and feeling hurt is part and parcel of the game of life just as much as it is in the game of football. People are often afraid of making contact emotionally with others since they're afraid that in doing so they would sustain injuries. Speaking up for yourself, expressing your point of view, saying what you want or don't want, defining acceptable boundaries for yourself in dealing with others are just some of the ways that we participate more fully in our lives, as a player. Not speaking up, not telling the truth, not setting boundaries, not making requests, not letting people know how we see things are ways that we sit on the bench.

I actually had the good fortune to experience playing the game of football completely differently. After high school and serving three years in the Marine Corps, I went to college and tried out for and made the football team, even playing varsity my freshman year. Somewhere along the way in the Marine Corps, I had made that distinction between hurt and injured. As a down lineman in college football, I will never forget those one-on-one practice drills, lining up against Glen Aidt. Coach Agler would blow the whistle and with all of our might, we exploded forward crashing into each other to gain the advantage. Sometimes Coach would have us go again, two or three times in a row, just to see the sparks between Glen and me. For me, however, it was actually stars, not sparks! But I couldn't wait to go again. Each time I felt the intense impact. They were damn good blocks, but they did not hurt because they were just part and parcel of the game.

During almost every football game, play will be stopped if a player is lying on the ground hurt being attended to by the trainer. The announcer is likely to comment that the trainer is determining whether there is an injury to the player or if the player is just hurt. Injury is defined essentially in physical terms such as break, tear, separation, sprain, whereas hurt refers essentially to pain. If the player does not have an injury, after waiting one play, he can return to the field of play even if he still feels pain. If the player does have an injury, he will not likely be cleared to play again until the injury has healed. Thus, the phrase "you can play the game hurt but not injured."

The distinction between hurt and injured is a very important one in the game of football. Consider for example that each time there is a play on the field opposing members of the team smash into each other with as much force and power as they can deliver. Tacklers attempt to punish the ball carrier and slam him into the ground as fiercely as possible. Blockers want to pancake tacklers to the ground to prevent them from tackling their runner. Now, if we were to stop the game for a moment after a play, and ask all of those football players, "Did that hurt?" the players might say something like, "No, that was a damn good block." "No, that was a jarring tackle. I really felt that one." The experience of a jarring tackle is certainly felt, but since it is so much part and parcel of the game of football, it may not be regarded as pain. That's not to say that the players don't ever feel pain. They may get up off the ground limping, and a teammate might say, "Shake it off, man," which is sort of a code that says move around, don't focus on it, and get mentally ready for the next play.

Our fearful minds flood us with thoughts of exaggerated risks of being hurt, harmed, injured. And when we really look at the mindtalk, we see that our fearful thoughts are almost all false and designed to hold us back from taking the risks of speaking our truth and taking bold action.

On any Saturday afternoon in football stadiums across the nation, there may be fifty to a hundred thousand people in the stadium watching 22 players on the field participating in the game. I have thought at times that must be about the same ratio of people who are players in life versus the benchwarmers of life making sure they don't get hurt. I don't know about you, but I intend to get in the game!

112

A tale of identity theft

Eli Mitchell

I have a confession to make; I'm guilty of identity theft.

Several years ago I faced the dreaded (by me) challenge of being deposed by two attorneys who were contesting a client's workers' compensation claim. This client, Danny C., was physically, mentally, and emotionally injured in a deadly industrial accident which was clearly the fault of his company.

During our eighteen months of psychotherapy sessions, I helped Danny to significantly reduce the intensity of his severe, classical symptoms of Posttraumatic Stress Disorder (PTSD). Even though Danny's case was strong and he deserved worker's compensation benefits (and his attorney would be present), I still was anxious about being deposed. Danny's future welfare depended on my presenting a convincing, winning argument on his behalf to the company lawyers.

Fortunately, the weekend before the deposition I attended an advanced Eye Movement Desensitization and Reprocessing (EMDR) workshop dealing with learning how to build-up one's personal resources. First, the workshop leader asked participants to get in touch with what resources, that is, self-skills and/or strengths we would like to amplify. Second, we were told to think of someone, anyone, who exhibits the characteristics we would like to strengthen in ourselves. This model "someone" could be a friend, family member, acquaintance, historical hero, a character from a novel, or even a TV or movie star. Third, the group was asked to think of demanding situations we might encounter when we would like to tap more fully into those personal resources.

Each of us participants then worked with a partner as our facilitator demonstrated how to utilize EMDR in this context. The EMDR process was used to positively reinforce our experience while we created in our mind's eye a challenging scene and then imagined behaving as if we had the desired strengths or skills to deal well with it.

I picked my role model to be Atticus Finch, the attorney played by Gregory Peck in the classic 1962 movie *To Kill A Mocking Bird*. Atticus was self-assured, assertive, soft-spoken, and a powerful advocate for his innocent client. The situation I chose to play out, of course, was the unnerving deposition awaiting me in the coming week.

To my surprise, I was even calm before I faced the "firing squad" during the actual deposition. Performing as a powerful advocate for Danny, I was able to pull up my basic resources of grit, firmness, and confidence. Unlike the way I handled lawyer pot shots (inquisitions) in the past, if I did not understand a question or if more time was needed to think, I would request that the question be asked again. Often the inquiring attorney would dismiss the question by saying, "Ah, forget it."

Atticus and I were victorious. Danny received the workers' compensation benefits he deserved.

Of course, I couldn't really use the qualities of a fictitious Atticus Finch, nor, the qualities of a real Gregory Peck. I can only use my own. I can, however, model somebody else in order to amplify what I already possessed within myself, my own resources, and my own potentialities.

Sometimes our self-identity limits us. In this case, it was my self perception was that I lacked the ability to sufficiently deal with those attorneys' pot shots. But through the EMDR process, I changed my unconscious, automatic sense of self and brought forward the grit, firmness, and confidence that I have exhibited many times in numerous other situations.

The gift of forgiveness

John Hoover

My first grade teacher's name was Miss Helen Reynolds. To me she was the "Wicked Witch of the West." She was just plain scary. She had no smile but did have lots of tightlipped impatience and a quick temper. Plus she boomed out harsh commands, effecting absolute control over all of us trembling kids.

My scariest experience with Miss Reynolds occurred in my reading group. There were three reading groups: the red birds, the bluebirds, and the sparrows. Everyone in the sparrows group was a terrible reader, and I was one of them—unable to comprehend what those jumbles of letters were supposed to mean.

Three decades later I would be diagnosed as having ADD and dyslexia, so it was no wonder I couldn't read or comprehend anything written. What's more, back in the 1940s when I was growing up, there were no programs for children needing special help, and no one had even heard of ADD or dyslexia.

Now, it was most often in the sparrows reading group that Miss Reynolds could really lose it. We had to take turns reading aloud, and when I made one too many mistakes she'd slam *Fun with Dick and Jane* into my face. No warning, just wham!

Needless to say my reading and comprehension was minimal at best and became diminished even more so by my terror of flocking with the three other sparrows in our reading group. Simply put, I couldn't understand anything I was reading. I learned words but they had no meaning, particularly as they joined up with other words to form sentences. I could read the words of a sentence. But if you asked me what I had just read, I had no clue! Reading became about the most abhorrent thing in my life.

By the time I was in junior high I rarely even tried to read homework assignments. Whatever I learned I learned from listening in the classroom; that is, if I wasn't spending my classroom time daydreaming about getting even with Miss Reynolds.

Since there were no diagnoses of ADD in my youth, I was diagnosed as "dummy." Yes, I was a dummy and I knew it. The sense I had of myself was that I was stupid, inept, and inferior. Everybody else was better than me, not just smarter, but better and more important, more valuable, and better off than me. My goal in every classroom was to be invisible, not to be called on. In summer school I would take classes to make up for the failing grades I had during the year. And somewhere in the back of my mind I would always be stewing about the despicable Miss Reynolds and how she instilled in me my hatred for reading anything.

I did graduate from high school with a C- or D+ average overall. Coming from a small town of 5,000 folks, a number of the kids that I graduated with started in the same first grade with me. And as in every class and every school, each student knows what group they belong to. There is that top group of kids, the next to the top group, the middle group, et cetera. and then there were those of us who either didn't belong or believed we didn't belong . . . anywhere.

As you might imagine, I had no interest whatsoever in going to college. I had a ghastly relationship with books. They made me very uncomfortable. Many people talk about how much they enjoy getting a good book and curling up on the couch for an evening of pure enjoyment. Just the thought of sitting on a couch reading a book would make my stomach churn. There was nothing that I read that was enjoyable, including comic books or magazines.

So I joined the Marine Corps. After my tour of duty I was able to go to college. Eventually, I was doing what I could to work around Miss Reynolds' hellacious impact from way back in the sparrows reading group. Although reading got easier, it never got enjoyable. I went on to complete my Masters degree followed by my Ph.D. from Ohio University in 1973.

A couple of decades later, my wife and I took my mother and father to a nursing home in my hometown of Upper Sandusky, Ohio, when it was necessary for both of them to have elder care. My mother had Alzheimer's, and my father had fallen down the cellar steps from a heart attack and cracked his neck against the cellar door.

On that first day my wife and I accompanied my mother and father to the cafeteria for their first meal in the nursing home. As we were walking into the cafeteria I heard: "Is that you, John Hoover?" I looked down and there sitting in her wheelchair was 95-year-old Miss Helen Reynolds. She extended her bony, brittle fingers out to me and took my hand. In a shaky little voice she said: "I heard your folks were coming. It sure is good to see you, John."

I introduced my wife, Sharon, to Miss Reynolds. Sharon was well aware of Helen Reynolds because of the many negative references I had made about her to just about anyone who would listen.

Helen said, "Lets see, you're in Knoxville, Tennessee, right?" "Wow," I said, "I'm impressed." "And your sister Miriam's in Huntsville, right? And Lois is in Florida?" "Wow," I said again, "what a memory you have."

By now Miss Reynolds was not only holding my hand but stroking the back of it and saying, "Oh, yes, I remember, you were just such a wonderful little boy." My mother, true to form, said, "Well that's because he had such a wonderful teacher." "No, no," said Miss Reynolds, shaking her head slightly back and forth. "Yes, you were. You were a wonderful teacher," protested my mother. Miss Reynolds brought her eyes up to mine and insisted, "No, actually she could get pretty crosswise, couldn't she John?" "Yes, she could," I whispered. With dim, tender eyes Miss Reynolds continued to peer into my eyes and asked, "Have you forgiven me?" I exhaled a long breath. "Yes, right now." With tears coming down our cheeks my wife, my mother and I listened as Miss Reynolds went on to tell about asking several of "her children" for forgiveness for the severity with which she'd treated them.

It was that very day that Miss Helen Reynolds became my greatest teacher. I have absolutely no doubt that no matter how, when, or where the lesson of forgiveness is taught, it is the most wonderful lesson of all. I wouldn't change a minute of my life to have had it any other way. Interestingly, I am now more at peace with reading than ever before.

Whenever Sharon and I visited my folks at Fairhaven Nursing Home we would also spend some time with Helen. And when we traveled to my hometown after both my folks had died, we'd still stop in to see Helen. The last time we stopped by it was a Fourth of July weekend. We were told that Helen had just died at the age of 99.

A SHORT STORY AND A POEM

MILK

Eli Mitchell

"Little Rose was gone, just like that," Dad said, snapping his fingers. "Crib death. There's no telling why it happens. It's a nightmare all of us parents have. Well, Son, for your mother and me it came true . . . it became so true."

Poor Dad was in one of those sighing moods so I sat as still as I could for a ten year old, poking my baseball glove. After fingering away tears, he continued, "You know, your mother hasn't been the same since. She worries about you boys so much. Too much." He shook his droopy head. "Way too much. Doesn't even want you growing boys out of her sight. Well, that's why, one night little Rosemary just died in her crib."

I tried to believe that story from the git-go. After all, Dad was a rare breed—an honest lawyer. But somehow I wasn't convinced. Besides, Mother didn't say that Rosemary died that way; she wouldn't say a thing. And I never knew her to cry about it either. She didn't cry about anything.

Doc Parker said she was melancholic, but he never saw her attack a dirty kitchen floor. With a vengeance. In fact she did all housework in a sinewy fury. Even on Sundays. Especially on Sundays. Dad would take my older brother, Nate, and me to church and Mother would clean the whole house, top to bottom, like a robot hung up in high gear.

Another thing Mother did with vigor was to pound into our heads that the world out the front door was to be feared. "Be on your guard" was her favorite motto. "Boys, take heed out there, you never know what you're up against" was a close runner-up. I remember many nights, after my brother and I were supposed to be asleep, she would peek in our bunkroom to check up on us. Seemed like just to see if we were still breathing.

Mother's declaration "nature is a brute" came across as so final that early on my brother and I abandoned all argument. The great outdoors for Mom was great only in the sense that the natural world was always a monstrous threat to our lives.

Now as far as most of our pet creatures went, Mom didn't seem to mind. We boys had quite a menagerie: hamsters, white mice, rabbits, dogs and cats, a raccoon named Bandido, and even a split tongued "talking" crow who never said a word. To my bewilderment, the only critter that couldn't stay awhile was the garter snake I captured in the back yard. Dad disappeared it at first sight.

My mind was muddled how Mother could be so afraid of her sons venturing out, especially into untamed territory, when she had sprung up smack in the middle of the mountains near Tellico Plains. As Dad told it many times, before Rosemary's death she flourished in those wild, pristine surroundings.

Mother was born on Mocking Crow Mountain in the farmhouse hand built by her parents. Growing up on this rugged homestead with three older brothers turned her into a wiry tomboy. Mom stacked up well with her brothers when hunting with a hand-me-down, double-barreled shotgun. In spite of shoulder bruises, like them she bagged plenty of rabbit, turkey, and ruffed grouse. Mother even built a fly rod from cane, tied her own flies, and using silk thread for line, she caught more speckled trout than all her brothers combined. Granddad said she was so tough she'd stand up to a circle saw.

There was one thing her brothers could tease their little sister about: she would not shoot a whitetail deer. No how come. Call her a sissy or a baby if you want, she just wouldn't do it.

Except for attending the Citico Creek Missionary Baptist Church twice a week, Mother didn't dress up until she was escorted to the junior prom by my father. That evening Dad found the lissome love of his life. During the June of their high school graduation, Reverend Honeycutt married them in Mother's living room. Since my parents were newlyweds during the Great Depression, they lived in my grandparents' house, intending to move as soon as they could afford their own place.

Marriage did not end Mother's love affair with her place on earth where God "touches the mountains, and they smoke." While my father law clerked in Tellico Plains, she worked and managed the family apple orchard for two autumns under my grandfather's guidance. One evening, near the end of the second fall harvest, Mom swayed down her long, narrow-topped ladder, and after leaning over a bushel basket and emptying her canvas bag of Rome Beauties, she announced to Dad, "In the words of Mr. Frost '. . .there may be two or three apples I didn't pick upon some bough. But I am done with apple-picking now.' We're goin' to get pregnant!"

After many months of "trying" to conceive (Dad said he didn't mind), Mom got pregnant and Rosemary was born—as easy as apple pie—in my parent's bedroom.

Four days following, father, mother and daughter went to the sun-rise service on Easter morning. Like her mother, Rosemary was robust and easygoing. Three months later, on the last Sunday in July, she was dead.

Right after Rosemary died, Mother felt smothered by the rural setting she had thrived in all her life. Now her home site was a constant sorrow. My parents lost heart to live in the mountains. With Rose's casket nested among belongings in the back of their pickup, Mom and Dad fled the highlands.

When they reached the town of Sweetwater, they laid Rosemary to rest in what Dad called the smooth and gentler soil of the Tennessee Valley. At her daughter's funeral, as Mother cast a handful of earth onto the coffin, she vowed never to praise God again.

From hearing Dad's retelling of the past, I understood why neither of my parents had ever returned to those mountains—the country of a terrible memory. But why was Mother so deathly afraid when her sons went out into any part of nature?

After I turned thirteen, the truth struck me on a summer day when Mother and I searched out her long-abandoned home place on Mocking Crow Mountain.

"Good grief, how did a country road get switched around like this?" Mother whined, her woeful blue eyes peering over the steering wheel. As we topped a hill, a shot of sun pierced the windshield and lit up her silver hair. "It shouldn't be this difficult to spot a Victorian house around here somewhere. Especially when it's sitting in the middle of a meadow. And bounded on three sides by an apple orchard."

Mother had taken several white-knuckle turns down dry roads that dead-ended either in a hollow or at the edge of a knob. Each time she got her new '55 Buick headed back out, we ate the dust our lumbering car had kicked up. Above the surrounding ridges, turkey buzzards glided sideways on updrafts of warm air.

"Thanks for bringing me out here," I said, deepening my teen voice. "I've never really been back in these mountains before. Always wanted to come."

"Yes, Son, I know. I've kept too tight a rein on you boys. And on myself." Her lips tightened. "Today, I'm changing . . . turning over a new leaf."

"Boy, I'm glad to hear that. You've never really wanted to get out very much, have you, Mom?"

Mother frowned, making her thin lips disappear.

My throat felt dry, more from uneasiness than from the heat and dust. Mom had long avoided taking this trip into the geography of her past. She even resisted driving in the countryside around Sweetwater, never mind the foothills. Bored by summertime, I had hounded her for weeks to take me to the mountains near Tellico Plains. I wanted to see where she had grown up. Persistence and a gawky height were in my corner. On the July morning that Mother gave into my relentless pressure, Nate was working at the carwash and Dad had gone to Atlanta on business. I had attacked when her usual buffers, my father and brother, were absent. Now I regretted my unfair tactics: isolate and overwhelm. Guilt settled over me like the dust we had just roiled.

"You're probably wondering 'why today', aren't you?" Mom asked. "Why, out of the blue, has my chicken mother decided to leave town and drive way over to a place she can't stand?"

"Well, I guess I 'bout twisted your arm off. I'm sorry. . . ."

"Nope," she snapped. "It's really Doctor Parker's fault. He's been saying for years I wouldn't get any better until I faced the past. 'Go back into those mountains and stare down the truth,' he said a hundred times. 'Get back on the horse that threw you.' So, here I am, exactly twenty years later, hopping on that damn horse again."

Pointing a quivery finger across my vision, she said, "And thar she blows. Hum, looks a little chewed-up by the weather."

More than chewed. Chunks of the outside walls had been bitten off and devoured. The farmhouse's dingy white paint was flayed, exposing rotten board siding. The whole structure was exhausted. The two-story house tilted so much to one side that it was propped against a dead oak. A sway-backed balcony hung low over the front porch; its gingerbread trim dangled like torn lace. Save the river rock chimney, still standing straight, the whole place was beaten down from neglect, brokenhearted.

Mom parked the car between two rows of barren apple trees, as close as she could get to the front yard. She killed the engine and asked, "You hear that real eerie cackle?" I nodded yes. "Around here they call it a wood hen; it's a big, beautiful, red crested bird. The Audubon name is Pileated Woodpecker." Showing interest, I nodded again as we got out of the car. We then picked our way through a briar patch to reach the remains of the house.

"The front door is half-open," I whispered. "Let's go in."

Ahead of me, Mother climbed up on the lopsided front porch. She was careful not to step where boards were missing or where they looked too rotten to hold her weight. A musty smell hung in the still air.

Mom tiptoed up to a wren's nest resting on a flagging joist. A black snake bolted out of the nest and slithered down the beam. To my astonishment Mother grabbed its tail, drew the snake back over her shoulder and cracked its squirming length like a bullwhip. Then she beat the snake's head against a post until it was a glob of red flesh. Blood splattered across the porch floor and red drops sprinkled my glasses. She slung the still writhing body through the thick air and it landed like a black hose some distance away in high weeds.

Mother slumped against the door frame, slid to the floor in a heap, and began to wail.

Moments went by before I recovered from the shock of witnessing my mother thrash the snake to death. I leaped onto the rickety porch and worked my way across the decay. I crouched beside her huddled body. Mother's wail had turned into sobbing.

"What's the matter, Mom?" I croaked.

She answered with a soft moan.

"Mom, black snakes are good snakes. They're harmless. Why . . . why'd you do that? They're good. They kill copperheads."

"They kill babies!" she yelled, bursting into tears again. I put my hand on her trembling back and the sobs began to die down. She crawled to the edge of the porch and threw up. As she was retching again and again, I got behind her and clutched her slim waist. This time Mother's lament was a whimper.

After straightening out her legs under her sundress, Mom leaned a bare shoulder against the wall, wiped her mouth and eyes with my handkerchief, and stared through the wavy heat into a pale and empty sky. Her voice was a monotone. "My baby girl died on a day just like today, all hot and sticky. We were over there, near that orchard." She pointed toward a hill covered with scruffy trees in even rows.

"Little Rose, she was only three months old. Your dad and I took her on a Sunday afternoon picnic. We were sitting under those sweet gums. . . . Dear God, we were so happy then. And Rosemary lived up to her name; her cheeks were rose and she smiled and cooed all the time. Such a delight. She was an angel."

Mother paused, deep in thought. I stood up and shook my leg to get out a cramp, then sat down and slid over as close as I could to her.

"Your dad went to pick some blackberries for dessert. The blackberry bushes weren't that far away; you could see berries everywhere. I stayed on the quilt and finished nursing Rose. Soon she fell asleep. I puffed up the quilt and laid her down."

Mother choked up but kept going. "I walked over to help Dad. I was only gone a second or two . . . just a few minutes. When we got back, there it was—a long black thing in her mouth! A snake! In her little mouth. Ooh."

Tears filled mother's eyes and began flowing down her cheeks. They fell drop by drop on her dress.

"Dad pulled the snake out but it was too late. Rose was BLUE, so blue and so limp. We tried and tried but we couldn't bring her back.

"Oh no, no," I said. "But why . . . why would a snake do that?"

"Milk," Mother groaned. "The snake was after my milk, still in her throat. She suffocated."

It was a while before Mother turned and looked straight at me. Her face was relaxed and her eyes were a clearer blue than I had ever seen. She drew her knees to her chin and rocked from side to side begging over and over, "Oh, God help me; God help me. Help me God." I put my arm around her shoulders and hugged her and rocked with her the best I could.

Doc Parker was right. Mother did get much better once she outbraved the truth. Her eyes stayed bright blue, she laughed a lot and wept openly when she felt like it. She talked Dad into hiring a cleaning woman so she would be freed up to go on long treks with the Cherokee Hiking Club. Besides teaching Nate and me how to fly fish, Mom insisted we attend a wilderness camp in the Great Smokies. The biggest surprise for all of us came the year after Nate was married. Unannounced, Mother showed up at church for the baptism of her twin granddaughters, Liza and Rosemary Kate.

Gathering stones for home

Eli Mitchell

Along the creek bed, mushrooms
are clusters of white sea coral.
Rock gardening,
we sling cobbles, river-worn,
toward our geometry
of spheres and ellipsoids,
clattering into a quilt.

A ruby-eyed terrapin stares.
Precious stones
and small animals peek, curious.
Mossy boulders know.

Among maidenhair fern
I tug a rock that won't
budge from sixty years
of root grasp; its cottonwood
stands tall toward
the sapphire blue above.

She points out a monolith:
"Pick up that one, right there."
"Whoa," I say. "Let's let the big ones
get away."
Our laughter pauses the tree frogs
of late August.

The stone-full hammock
swinging between,
we tote our harvest home.

ABOUT THE AUTHORS

Eli Mitchell

I was born in Greenville, South Carolina, on July 18, 1941. In August of 1947, my mother died, a heartbreaking event for me (see "Shedding the 'nice boy' drama," page 96). Subsequently, my father married my wicked step-mother (1948-1953), then his third wife, my loving step-mother, in 1957.

After my sophomore year at Greenville High School, I attended a boarding school—Christ Episcopal School for Boys—in the mountains near Asheville, North Carolina.

During my senior year at this prep school (1959), everyone in my class took an occupational interest test. My highest score on this test was "Clinical Psychologist," and it was at that moment that I began to consider psychology as a lifelong profession.

In 1959, I began my undergraduate studies at Duke University. While there another "aha moment" occurred while watching the movie, *David and Lisa,* a love story between a young man and woman who were both patients in a mental institution. The resident psychologist, played by Howard Da Silva, counseled the couple with great compassion and understanding. I found myself deeply relating to the psychologist and visualized myself being like him and doing the kind of work he was doing.

After college graduation in June 1963, I attended Navy Officer Candidate School in Newport, Rhode Island, and was commissioned an officer on November 22, 1963, the day President John F. Kennedy was assassinated.

Upon being commissioned, I unexpectedly got exactly the military orders I wanted: "ship-out aboard a small combat ship that travels widely." I served three years as an Ensign and then a Lieutenant (junior grade) on board the *USS Valcour,* a flag ship for the Commander of the Middle East Force. Throughout my military service, we "traveled widely" throughout the Indian Ocean, Red Sea, and Persian Gulf. It was quite an adventure for a young man from South Carolina.

After I completed my service in the Navy, I continued my explorations, traveling throughout Europe for nine months. But my calling pulled at me, so I returned to the U.S. and started clinical psychology graduate school at University of Tennessee, Knoxville in September of 1967. During this period of my life, I protested the Vietnam War on the UTK campus, in Washington D.C., and in San Francisco.

In 1974, I earned a Ph.D. in Clinical Psychology from the University of Tennessee Knoxville. My dissertation was on *Induced Fantasy*, a precursor to research on Guided Imagery. In that same year I was licensed as a Clinical Psychologist, State of Tennessee. I trained at the Gestalt Therapy Institute in Los Angeles, California during the early 1970s, and in 1974 graduated from Advanced Gestalt Therapy Training, Pine River Center Atlanta, Georgia.

Also in 1974, I began my psychology practice that continues today. From 1974 to 1984 I served as the Founding Director of Gestalt Center South. Through GCS I trained mental health professionals, and sponsored trainings in Neuro-Linguistic Programming, Ericksonian Hypnotherapy, and Strategic Family Therapy. In addition, I have worked with war veterans and World Trade Center trauma survivors.

Other significant trainings in which I've participated include Pesso Psychomotor Therapy, Psychotherapy: A Jungian Perspective, Eye Movement Desensitization and Reprocessing (EMDR), Holothropic Breathwork, Critical Incident Stress Management, Jungian Analysis, and courses at Esalen Institute.

In 1977, I married Lucy Oakley and gained an eight-year-old daughter, Tina. Together Lucy and I were baptized (2000) by Tina into the Knoxville Church (nondenominational) where I served as a Deacon for eight years.

Why I do what I do

I do what I do because it's in my blood. A (many-greats-back) grandfather was the first missionary sent from England (1702) to the Province of South Carolina by The Society for The Preservation of The Gospel In Foreign Parts.

The grandfather I knew growing-up was an Episcopal Priest and, for awhile as a child, I thought he was God Almighty. However, the idea of following in his minister footsteps was much too tame so, when I was a preteen, I made up stories about being a missionary in Africa, fighting off crocodiles and grizzlies. Eventually, however, I decided to help folks fight off the demons of the mind as a psychotherapist.

Why, all these 36 years, have I relished being a psychotherapist? To paraphrase Richard Bach, it's because I have been able to teach best what I've needed to learn the most.

Blessed with my Christian missionary heritage and the benefits (such as they were) of early trauma, I'm called out to love God with all my heart, soul, mind, and strength, and to love my neighbor as myself (Mark 12:29-31).

When I serve others as a psychotherapist, I am served. There's a myriad of personal rewards to assisting my "neighbors" in overcoming addictions, traumas, and the challenges of our (extremely) worldly Western culture that's filled with greed, sex, and violence. I get to share in their victories and, sometimes, glimpse into their souls. I am also fed by the rich life stories of clients, some of which I can convert to poetry or fiction.

Even when I suffer and fail in my professional pursuits, I still gain personally if I can turn these dynamics into opportunities for personal growth. Most importantly, when I'm on my game, I can coach others along their own spiritual path.

The Amish say, "We believe in letting our light shine, but not shining it in the eyes of other people."

So do I.

John Hoover

I grew up in Upper Sandusky, Ohio, a small farming community of 5,000. Believing I had no need (or aptitude) for further education, after I graduated from high school in 1957, I enlisted in the Marine Corps. One day while aboard a Navy troop transport ship as part of a battalion of Marines maintaining a presence in the Mediterranean Ocean, I had an epiphany (see "Learning to ride the horse in the direction that the horse is going," page 100), and my entire world view radically shifted. For some reason I was drawn to the ship's library, and in a state of inspiration I actually felt a real desire to learn for the very first time in my life.

In among the books in that wonderful little library was literature on correspondence courses including enrollment forms. That morning I enrolled in a correspondence course: Introduction to Psychology. I had just declared my profession. I was going to be a psychologist!

After serving my three-year enlistment, I enrolled at Otterbein College in Westerville, Ohio. While there, I met and married my wife Sharon and earned a B.A. in Psychology in 1964. Following that, I secured my M.A. in Human Relations at The Ohio University, Athens, Ohio, in 1966. I did my APA approved Psychology Internship at the University of Texas, Austin, Texas, 1970-1972, and in 1973, I received my Ph.D. in Counseling Supervision at The Ohio University. I was a psychologist!

After holding several teaching and counseling positions, I, along with Sharon and our two daughters, Karin and Elizabeth, moved to Knoxville, Tennessee, in 1977 so Sharon could begin a Doctoral program in Speech Pathology.

In 1978, I opened a private practice of psychology at the Center for Psychology and Counseling in Knoxville, counseling with individuals and couples. I co-led Gestalt training weekends for mental health practitioners, and I created and conducted workshops for teachers, managers, organizations, businesses, and government agencies. In addition, with Dr. Vergil Metts, I co-created the *Emotionally Intelligent Manager* workshop that Dr. Metts and I have presented throughout the United States and Mexico.

Additional training experiences that have significantly influenced my work include Neuro Linguistic Programming (NLP), Eye Movement Desensitization and Reprogramming (EMDR), Enneagram Trainings, Holotropic Breathwork, and The More To Life Program.

Why I do what I do

My day job is my private practice of psychotherapy. When I work with my clients I feel enriched. I get to connect in a special way to people who feel safe enough to be vulnerable with me as they explore their hopes and fears. They trust me to respect their vulnerability without judgment, and I feel privileged to be in partnership with them in this way. My wife, Sharon, says that I am able to say things to people that others couldn't get away with because, she says, I have no malice in what I say. People know that I am *for* them.

I love finding that connection with my clients that is deeply personal and yet professional, where the sense of me and thee is equal, and only our roles are different. At the end of a session, I feel grateful for our connection and excited about the steps that were taken during that time.

In addition to my therapy practice, I love to present trainings that I have created or helped to create and witness the shifts that take place there. I have been privileged to help create and present *The Emotionally Intelligent Manager* workshop with one of the most brilliant, competent, compassionate men I have ever known—Dr. Vergil Metts, an Organizational Development Psychologist and President of Impact Associates.

OUR PROFESSIONAL PATHS

Our work together

John: I recall meeting you, Eli, in 1978 when we were both volunteer psychologists for the Child Abuse Review Team. Our team met to hear case presentations of possible child abuses and to make recommendations on actions to be taken. After one of the meetings, you invited me to your office building on Chambliss Avenue.

Eli: I remember it well. We sat on the front steps of my office, and after spending a couple of hours with you, I invited you to consider opening up your practice there with me and two other psychologists. You accepted, and we've been tight friends and fellow travelers ever since.

John: Yes, we became close friends almost immediately. At that time, you, Dr. Angela Masini, and Dr. Karen Swander, the other psychologists at the Chambliss Office, were also leaders in the Gestalt Center South Training Organization. I became associated with the Center staff when Dr. Masini and Dr. Swander went off the training staff, and you and I ran the Gestalt training programs for a number of years.

Eli: And I believe that our collaboration in the writing of this book springs from a natural progression of our professional, personal, and spiritual growth having been intertwined all of these 32 years that we have been in cahoots.

John: After all those years, Eli, I continue to be grateful for your personal honesty, your openness, your capacity to feel deep empathy, all of which have blended so well with your rich grounding in the Gestalt work. You have been a great teacher and model for me, passing along many things by example that you're probably not even aware of.

Eli: Wow, thanks, my friend. That's a lot to let in. And I want you to know that I've been able to integrate and pass on the extraordinary knowledge and valuable insights you've shared with me thanks to your insightful, non-judgmental mentoring. Being a coach, an innovator, and a creator and designer of new models, especially in the field of conflict resolution, you have helped me really broaden my horizons and pass along your wisdom to my clients and workshop participants.

John: Eli, I think we have a mutual admiration society going here.

Eli: Works for me!

Our collaborations

- Gestalt Center South trainings for mental health professionals
- *Assertion and Sensitivity Training* for TVA's Watts Bar Nuclear Power plant construction managers
- Counseling veterans at the Knoxville Vet Center
- Breathwork and rebirthing retreats at Pawleys Island, South Carolina

FUTURE PATHS

The Elders Speak Events

The Elders Speak Forums

The Elders Speak Forums are gatherings of people who would like to have Dr. Mitchell, Dr. Hoover, or both meet with them. Both Hoover and Mitchell are experienced group facilitators and group leaders. They will answer questions of a psychological, spiritual, interpersonal, and intrapersonal nature. They will facilitate discussions on any of the topics in *The Elders Speak* book or on any psychological topic the group chooses to discuss.

The Elders Speak Seminars

The Elders Speak Seminars are three-hour presentations with audience participation. Most presentations include a Power Point and handouts, provided by The Elders. Topics include: The Uniting Power of Conflict; The Enneagram Personality Types; The Power of Intentional Thought; Enlivening Your Life; and Dealing with Stress.

The Elders Speak Coaching

The Elders Speak Coaching is usually done by phone consultations on a weekly basis with Dr. Hoover who does both personal coaching with individuals and business coaching with owners and executives.

Author contact information

Dr. Mitchell: Phone: 865. 588.1923, ext. 106

Dr. Hoover: Phone: 865.250.0927

Website: www.TheEldersSpeak.com

LaVergne, TN USA
21 November 2010
205481LV00007B/4/P